Those unschooled minds:

home-educated children grow up

Julie Webb

The Educational Heretics Series

Published 1999 by Educational Heretics Press
113 Arundel Drive, Bramcote Hills, Nottingham NG9 3FQ

British Cataloguing in Publication Data

Webb, Julie
       Those unschooled minds:
       home-educated children grow up
       1. Home schooling - Great Britain
       I Title
       371 '. 042 ' 0922 ' 41

ISBN   1-900219-15-8

Design and production: Educational Heretics Press

Cover design: Bird cage motif inspired by a quotation from Philip Jackson's book *Life in Classrooms:*
"For all of the children some of the time, and for some of the children all of the time, the classroom resembles a cage from which there is no escape."

Printed by Mastaprint Ltd, Sandiacre, Nottingham, NG10 5HU

Contents

In memory of my father, Ron Tupper

Acknowledgments

I am deeply grateful to all those who gave up their time to be interviewed for this book and talked with such honesty, clear-sightedness and gusto about the experience of home education. (To preserve the confidential nature of our discussions, all of them appear with pseudonyms, false beards etc.)

Thank you to Mimi Tupper and Andrew Hearsey, who were kind enough to comment on the first draft. Thank you, also, to the *Society of Authors* for the research grant from its Kathleen Blundell Trust - the book would not have appeared without it. And thank you to Howard Gardner, whose book on multiple intelligences, *The Unschooled Mind* gave me the idea for the book's title.

Finally, I would like to acknowledge the huge influence on my thinking generated by the work of A.S.Neill, John Holt and Roland Meighan - inspiration for a personal philosophy of life and learning as well as a sane vision of how alternatives to conventional education could equip our children and grandchildren to find fulfilment and happiness in a rapidly changing world.

Julie Webb
Summer 1999

Introduction

It is more than 20 years now since the ground-breaking support group for British home educators, *Education Otherwise (EO)*, was set up, and people still say to me in amazement, *"But isn't that illegal? Children **have** to go to school!"*

They do not, of course. It is education itself that is compulsory, not education in school, and thousands of parents over the last 20 years have seized the opportunity, which the law affords them, to invent a custom-made education for their family. By exercising imagination and ingenuity, they have been able to extend their children's educational horizons beyond the cramped confines of a nationally prescribed curriculum *"delivered"*, (to use the current management-speak), in not very inspiring surroundings to a group unvaried in age, and preoccupied with the petty observances which maintain the hierarchy and discipline of the conventional classroom.

An outrageously generalised vilification of the system, many readers will say, and there are, without doubt, some excellent schools, staffed by thoughtful teachers more concerned to foster a child's unique talents than to encourage conformity to a 'good pupil' stereotype. But my experience of a range of primary and secondary schools in several LEAs -from the differing perspectives of parent, learning support assistant and researcher - strongly suggests that to find such a teacher or school is a matter of rare luck.

The people who are the subject of this book, home educated for part, or all, of their years of compulsory education, come from families with many different reasons for ditching the orthodox structure. The common factor in their approach is the intention of replacing the *"one size fits all"* philosophy with learning that emerges from the abilities and interests of the individual, deepening and expanding as the child matures. This learning is partly planned and partly serendipitous, and it can take place anywhere: using the computer-based resources of a large library or Internet cafe; as an apprentice in the working world; in the home of an artistic or musical friend keen to pass on their skills; at local drama club rehearsals or junior sports team practices;

even in schools and colleges on a part-time basis, or an *Education Otherwise* get-together. The possibilities are literally endless since the world and the student are constantly changing.

This contemporary kind of home-based education, scarcely at home at all in many cases, is very far removed from the historical image of privileged children sitting day after day in the nursery or schoolroom with a governess, often sheltered from life's realities and knowing from an early age the path they are expected to follow. Modern home education really took off with the founding of *EO* in 1977 by a group of pioneering parents under the guidance of the social and environmental visionaries Dick Kitto and Stan Windass, and the alternative educationalist Roland Meighan. I hope my discussion of interviewees' reflections on their experiences will shed an incidental light on the growth of a movement with some fairly revolutionary implications for standard educational thinking.

Although the numbers known to be home educating in those very early days scarcely reached double figures, and local networks of moral support and legal advice did not exist as they do now, families considering home education in the year 2000 may have broadly similar concerns to their predecessors. Will their children be able to get satisfying jobs, make friends, raise families, enjoy their leisure time? Do they need to jump through the conventional academic hoops to achieve their aims, and if so, how can this be done out of school? How important is it to read by a certain age? What resources are there for home educating on a low income? How on earth do parents get any time to themselves?

Fortunately, there are several studies and personal accounts of home education that families can turn to for encouragement and reassurance. This book, my own contribution to a growing body of information on something that could benefit many more children than currently have access to it, is based on interviews with 20 home educated people. They are now in their twenties or thirties except for one, a man who taught himself while travelling round Europe with his family's circus, who is somewhat older. I first spoke to about a quarter of them as teenagers in the early 1980s. Apart from one person who replied to a paragraph about the study in the *Times Educational Supplement*, and another whom I met through a friend, I got in touch with all of them through *Education Otherwise*, of which their families had been, or were still, members.

I wanted to find out what sort of lives they were leading now, and hear their reflections on the process of home educating, and I thought it would be interesting from the point of view of educational and social history to see whether they would contemplate home educating their own children. The later chapters, those examining home educated people's adult lives, a topic not much investigated so far in this country, are longer and more detailed than the earlier ones, which look at the process of home education, an area which has been rather better covered, (see References). I have tried to present a warts-and-all analysis of what my interviewees told me, believing that discussion of the inevitable difficulties encountered, as well as being helpful to parents and other educators, gives the validity of realism to some generally very positive findings.

****

Chapter one

One size fits all?

"Recent research in neuroscience and cognitive development has resulted in a new understanding of the process of learning, based on the view of the brain as a complex, highly adaptive, self-organising system. The new understanding recognises the active construction of knowledge, in which all new information is related to past experience in a constant search for patterns and meaning; the importance of experiential learning; of diverse learning styles involving multiple intelligences; and of the emotional and social context in which learning takes place."

Fritjof Capra, 'The language of nature',
Resurgence, no.192, Jan/Feb 1999

In other words, the theoretical world of contemporary science, and educational psychology in particular, has caught up, just about, with the real-world practice of home educators over the last two decades - practice which acknowledges, sometimes instinctively and sometimes in an explicit, fully articulated, fashion, that the features Capra describes can be better realised through individual learning programmes than through the standardised processing of the school system.

Future chapters will examine the ways in which these aspects of a more flexible approach to learning were tackled by the families of my interviewees. Here, I am concerned with the reasons why families took the remarkable, and daring, step of rejecting the schools' 'one size fits all' philosophy in favour of something which, as we have seen, is only now beginning to ruffle the fringes of mainstream academic thinking. Is it possible to answer in a British context the question posed by the excellent and stimulating American home-educating magazine, *Growing Without Schooling (GWS)* in *GWS* 120, p19:

> *"Plenty of people complain about the schools and recognise their children are unhappy there - what characterises those parents who go the extra mile and take their children out?"*

What made your parents consider home education?

(Note: Each of the sub-headings that follow are based on one of the questions interviewees were asked.)

It is clear from interviewees' recollections that in most cases there was no simple, or single, reason for opting out - a wide range of considerations was involved. These included the obvious ones such as the educational and emotional needs of the child, and a perception that these were not being well catered for in school, or would not be were the child to go there, and some less obvious factors such as family lifestyle and ideology.

Though none of those I interviewed came into this category, it appears that some heavily religious families in Britain and, more particularly, the States, have adopted home education for similar reasons to the old aristocratic families. These were essentially their own forms of the social, moral and intellectual control which the majority of home educators are intent on avoiding - causing a certain amount of concern to those of us who believe that education should promote free thought and as wide an experience of the world as possible.

The opportunity to talk to three lots of siblings emphasised the uniqueness of the circumstances affecting each decision even within the same family, and reinforced my sense of the downright oddness of expecting conventional classroom situations to serve individual educational needs. Flora and Harriet Frampton, now in their mid-20s and still living in the West Country, where they grew up, both said that the family's image of being *"different"*, due to a lifestyle unusual at that time, was a shared factor in their unhappiness at school:

> *"My sister, my younger brother and I all came out for different reasons. We were vegetarians and that wasn't*

common then, and my Dad was disabled as well so I got a lot of teasing about that. At that age I couldn't cope with it, I was very defensive about it. I couldn't understand why they did it." Flora

Harriet also commented on the teasing but mentioned an extra reason in her case for leaving school:

"I went up to the secondary school and I just didn't feel that I was learning anything, just messing about in the classroom all the time. I probably could have just stayed there and not learnt anything. I was unhappy there, I didn't like it...everyone used to take the Mick a bit; a few little bullies and that, there. My Mum had already got Flora out of school and she said 'You can come out'."

Flora explained what she thought her parents hoped to achieve by taking the children out of school:

"They were aiming to make us happier and give us a, not a really strict education, not down one road, or a narrow approach as the National Curriculum might do."

This interplay of specific school circumstances or local educational options, parents' educational philosophy and the influence of lifestyle, cropped up again and again in the interviews, with varying weights attached to each factor. It might be interesting to disentangle them and look at them separately, as far as this is possible.

Life in school

Many of the interviewees, who had at some time been to school, had vivid memories of unhappiness there, or a sense of not fitting in, and had themselves played a large part in the family decision-making about home education. Three in particular forced the issue by exhibiting symptoms of what the educational establishment calls 'school phobia':

"I started going to secondary school like everyone else at 11, and had a very extreme reaction to it. I'd been very happy at my junior school - there weren't any problems - but I changed from a very small primary school to a huge comprehensive and I think the shock of that change was quite hard for me to take." Kate Dixon

"Those things are very damaging - the social structure that comes up in schools. I was all right at primary school, all right-ish, and when I got to secondary school, being physically smaller is, I guess, what started it off. It can be very self-perpetuating - once you are the class scapegoat it can be very hard to get out of that situation."

Jim Merriman

One of these three supported the often-expressed view that 'phobics' react the way they do because of home, rather than school, circumstances, though she felt that the school's treatment of her had exacerbated the problems that originated with her family:

"When I was at primary school it was a very nice place to be really but my relationship with my Mum and Dad was very difficult and I was just a very, very insecure child. I didn't believe Mum would be there to pick me up, and I didn't want to leave her. I changed to a middle school when I was nine and that was when it really got bad because the teachers there were very - well, today I suppose you'd call it abusive - but in those days it was standard practice, things like carrying me in by my hair, kicking and screaming. And that was when I just wouldn't, couldn't, go back in and that was when I had the time in hospital."

Emma Morgan

Parents' educational philosophies

Educational philosophies were generally variations on the common theme of home-based learning as a better vehicle for individual development than school:

"I think my parents had some reservations about the education system. My Dad's a psychiatrist and my Mum's a birth teacher and is really involved in birth issues. I think it was the uniform education they were concerned about, and kind of restrictive education as well. For example, history is always written from a white, English, point of view, rather than whatever else."

Paul Todd

"What made my Mum think of doing it was my older brother. When it came to the time he was going to start school, she

didn't like the thought of him going off and sitting in a classroom while we were going off and doing all these other interesting things which she felt were just as educational, but in a different way, and less restrictive. She always says it came naturally to her - she knew she was doing what she felt was right, and she had the confidence to do it."

Pippa Hawkins

Parents' own school experiences were, inevitably, an influence on their educational philosophy:

"My Dad had a very hard time at school, got bullied and all that." Olivia Kirby

"My parents are old hippies. Neither of them had a good time at school even though they both did very well academically and went on to higher education. They hated it, thought it was a horrible place." Mandy Wood

Many of these parents' school experiences were as teachers as well as pupils:

"Dad teaches English as a foreign language and he didn't have very much respect for the system anyway."

Olivia Kirby

Almost half the interviewees had one or more parents who was a teacher, and these tended to be the families where all the siblings had been given the option of home-based education:

"They were both former teachers. My father was a lecturer and my mother taught at school. They had both retired when they started teaching me...the three oldest ones all went through school. The rest of us are adopted and I have one older sister, and from her and me all the way down we've all been home educated." Charlie Curtis

Mandy Wood's 'old hippy' Mum had also taught:

"She'd been a primary school teacher - she said she used to get kids coming in bright-eyed and bushy-tailed, and leaving at 16 as sullen and bad-tempered adults. She said, 'Somewhere in the middle it's gone wrong'. She didn't want that to happen to me."

Grace and George Gordon's mother, who happened to be around when I was interviewing and educated both her children to FE College level, commented on one of the aspects of conventional education that had bothered her as a teacher - schoolchildren's lack of control of their own learning:

> *"That's something that children suffer from - they don't know what's coming next. They just do this work, do that work, but they see no structure behind it. It's just what you've got to do."*

Laurence Hammond's parents, both teachers, had also come to hold new ideas about education through their working experience:

> *"So much time and effort seemed to be wasted...and my parents believe in teaching people who want to learn. That's why my Dad went into adult education: the people that come to him are people who've chosen to be there."*

The important point about the frequency of such comments is not that these parents have the wherewithal, in terms of resources, confidence and techniques, to educate their own children, but that they have the *desire* to: they've found the system they were trained for wanting, and are looking for ways to do something strikingly different.

Way of life

Some decisions to home educate were the result of gradual changes in families' thinking about how they wanted to live, often involving self-employment or a greater measure of self-sufficiency - changes which made school education a less automatic choice:

> *"Being out of mainstream and working - they set up their own business in candle-making - they couldn't see the point of doing their own stuff and then suddenly having to be tied down to school timetables so they decided they could probably do just as good a job at home."*   Mandy

> *"Education Otherwise had just started then and my parents were friends with Dick Kitto, who founded it. It coincided with us leaving London and moving to the country so it was a logical point to do it."*   Chloe Cassell

An article by Liz Andrew in *Weekend Telegraph* (9.01.99), about three sisters, Cadi, Linnhe and Bryony Catlow, who have developed an internationally famous animation company in their teens, described the family lifestyle:

> *"What makes their success so remarkable is that the three girls spent their childhood in an isolated house 1000 feet up a mountainside in North Wales. The twins were taken out of primary school at the age of six, Bryony did not even start school, and they have no paper qualifications ... 'Our parents never placed much emphasis on exams', says Cadi. They would say, 'You don't have to bother, you can do that sort of thing when you're 40'. Instead, the girls built dens, signalled with semaphore and bumped around in an electric buggy their father had converted from an old lawn mower. The family grew as much of their own food as possible, and the girls remember being outdoors nearly all the time... Self-expression was approved of at all times."*

Sometimes the reason for embarking on home education is a strictly practical one, such as apparent 'school phobia', and is unrelated to a particular choice of lifestyle. This tends to be the case in families where only one child is home educated and the rest have gone to perfectly conventional schools.

Daniel Scheaffer's parents decided to educate him at home because he had medical problems which would have made attendance at school very difficult: hypersensitivity to temperature change, and a form of autism which prevented him communicating and led to frequent loss of temper through frustration. Meeting him now, a charming, thoughtful, much-travelled and excessively talkative man of 34, one has to recognise that the alternative, a special school or similar institution, could hardly have been an improvement on what he received at home in terms of enabling him to overcome his difficulties.

For Edward Proctor, (my oldest interviewee and now, I guess, in his early 60s), keen to learn and rather a fish out of water as part of a travelling circus and variety act, there really no alternative to teaching himself:

"The members of the family just travelled, seldom in a place for more than a week. From time to time I went to live with my grandparents, who were retired and settled by that time. I would go to the local school when I was there, but that was constantly being broken up, and I actually left school before I was 13. From then onwards anything in terms of education was up to me. We had an acrobatic act, so I did the odd tricks and things that were required and I used to go to the theatre in the morning, mainly to practise the piano. The rest of the day I would tramp round wherever we were, go to a museum, reference library, places of interest. Work very often consisted of maybe ten, twenty, minutes in an evening so I had plenty of time to learn."

It is interesting that Edward and the two others who taught themselves with virtually no adult support, Kate Dixon and Emma Morgan, have the most generally negative attitude towards home education today, despite a recognition of some of its benefits for them personally. Perhaps this indicates that successful home education is, ideally, well integrated into the family lifestyle, a joint enterprise between children and parents with commitment and enthusiasm on each side.

How did your parents know they could legally do it?

Most interviewees were unable to answer this question.

"I'm not sure how they knew they could do it, but they'd always been members of EO."   Flora

The issue does not appear to have been particularly important to their parents, in marked contrast to the usual reaction of members of the public to the idea. This may suggest that these home educators were of a more anarchic turn of mind than those to whom the possibility of doing things differently from the schools might not occur. This was undoubtedly true in some cases, the Woods for example. It might also imply that worries about how their children's educational welfare could best be served overrode other considerations:

*"They can't remember how they got to know it was a legal option, but they remember they decided first of all to teach me at home and **then** found out it was legal."*   Olivia

"My parents didn't know it was legal to do that and it was very difficult because we didn't have any support from the council."   Kate

Those parents who, like the Framptons, were early members of *Education Otherwise*, were presumably familiar with the law right from the start, though some went on to challenge its interpretation, as a later section, discussing answers to a question about relations with the Local Education Authority, (LEA), demonstrates.

How much choice did you get about home education?

Offering a choice was an important part of most parents' view that school attendance should be voluntary, based on a belief that learning depends on self-motivation. This seems to be a general principle, since national consensus among the membership regards it as one of the three formal aims of EO to *"establish the primary right of children to have full consideration given to their wishes and feelings about their education"*.

Of those children who never went to a conventional school, or only for a period less than a year - 8 out of the 20 interviewees - most appeared to feel they had had some choice in the matter and were neither home educated against their will, nor prevented from trying school out of curiosity when they wanted to do so:

*"They always left it very open that we **could** go to school - and my middle brother did go when he was nine."* Laurence

"Apart from five months when I was 14, I was home educated all my life. I was very happy with it but you get all these stories from the other kids: 'Oh yes, school's great!', so I thought I'd try it in case I'd made the wrong choice. So I said to my parents 'I've thought about it, I'd really like to try it', and they said 'OK, off you go'."   Mandy

Those who went to school for longer periods also felt they'd been instrumental in making their own educational choices:

"It was just a question of seeing how it went and seeing what I wanted to do as the years passed. I always had the option to go back in when I wanted to."   Chloe

"We moved to East Anglia so that I could go to A.S. Neill's free school, Summerhill, but then my parents didn't like the look of it very much, and the travelling was awkward and it was difficult if you were a day pupil. And I was quite stroppy when I was little and I didn't really want to go. I would have possibly gone to a local primary school if it was in walking distance. I think it was to do with being able to walk home if I didn't like it. At that time I never actually went to school - I just decided I didn't like the idea of it. I didn't like the idea of being told what to do or how to do things. I probably wouldn't have gone to school for longer, except that when I was 11 we moved up to North Yorkshire so that we could go to the Steiner School at Botton. They felt that they would be happy with me going to school there, and I agreed. It was a shared decision. I thought that it was time for me to go. I felt ready then, and I didn't when I was younger." Heather Taylor

"I never wanted to go to school when I was that age (primary) *- it never occurred to me at all. I had friends that were at school and I had friends that weren't at school - it never worried me."*   Pippa

There was one exception to this general picture of shared decision-making:

"I think it was all decided. I enjoyed most of it. It was different but it was the thing I grew up with so I never thought about it. At 11 I just accepted it, didn't question why. I still accept it - now I'm older I still haven't asked them, 'What made you decide to take me out?'"   Charlie

How did the LEA behave?

Treatment of interviewees' families by the LEA varied from the rather intimidating to a complete lack of contact. These two experiences represent opposite ends of the spectrum:

"They got a lot of problems at first...the authorities definitely didn't like it there at all. They came every six months. I remember being really nervous."   Flora

"I didn't get any inspection at all. I don't know why. We slipped the net. They caught up with the next one along - they were just aware of my presence as I went back into the system. I know he did come round to see my sister from time to time but it was never a problem."   Chloe

Most families, in the interests of a quiet life and possible resource benefits, established cordial relations with the local authorities:

"We had a very, very nice man where we were, the inspector. He'd been home educated himself. He didn't go to school until he was about nine. So he was very helpful and used to bring us things he'd got from schools, like paints and books. He'd come for coffee and he'd say, 'Are you still happy Heather?' and I'd say, 'Yes'. He was the one who pointed out a lot of the loopholes - like 'You have to have an education but it's not specified anywhere what it is'. I think otherwise it might have been harder for them to feel that they were doing the right thing."   Heather

"We had an inspector who used to come round and make sure we were learning to read and write, just to make sure it wasn't some kind of New Age hippy parents. She was lovely." Olivia

Mandy Wood's parents, on the other hand, decided to deny the LEA access to the family home on the basis of their own interpretation of the law. (This interpretation has since become recognised as correct and incorporated into EO's legal guidelines.)

"The authorities took an erratic interest in my education. I can remember in Leeds, where we used to live, we had a school adviser come round a few times a year, to check out how I was doing. He was fine - I liked him. Then we moved up to the Dales and my Dad re-read the Education Act and said, 'There's nothing in here that says that they have the right to visit.' My Dad doesn't like having people looking over his shoulder telling him what to do anyway. He was doing a good job, and he said, 'I'll tell them I'm doing a good job but I don't want them up here'."

After several fruitless attempts to visit, they eventually gave up, partly reassured perhaps by Mandy's mother's teaching qualification.

As for the next generation of home educators, Sally James, herself home educated and intermittently home educating her own daughter, reported that:

> *"They never got in touch at all. I wrote to the school, I kept stuff that she was doing - we never got a thing. I think they've got enough on their plates without chasing up people who know what they're doing."*

This may indicate a gradual social effect, that LEAs are beginning to regard people like Sally as the real experts in home education, or, as she also implies, that a busy city authority with its fair share of educational problems is only too glad to give apparently responsible parents a low priority.

In answer to the question posed in GWS then, it appears from these accounts that the factor triggering a family decision to home educate is frequently parents' knowledge of the school system as teachers. They understand how much time is wasted on routine, and how children's innate curiosity can be eroded, and sometimes finally extinguished, by boredom. They are confident of providing a stimulating alternative. Those, such as the families of the 'phobics' mentioned earlier, who home educate for other reasons, and are perhaps uncertain at first, can take courage from these insiders who know exactly what it is their children are missing.

Chapter two

Lighting a fire

"Education is not the filling of a pail,
but the lighting of a fire. " W. B. Yeats

This concept of learning - inspiring and equipping people for a lifetime of discovery as opposed to providing them with a finite package of information - underlies much of what my interviewees told me about the content of their home education and how it originated, although many opted in to the 'package' culture for the purpose of obtaining qualifications. Many of the activities in which they find satisfaction as adults, whether paid or unpaid work, hobbies or social pursuits, have roots in something they encountered through the opportunities of the unlimited world of home-based education.

This seems to be particularly true in the field of creativity, an area more unsuited than most to the strict time constraints and regimented syllabus of the school day. The businessman, pianist and composer, Sir Ernest Hall, talked about his own schooling on the programme, *Another String*, suggesting how important it is that creative pursuits are not seen in orthodox examination terms:

"There was no music on the curriculum, thank God! I'm always terrified that once education gets its hands on something, it becomes a subject, in which people learn to fail. "   Radio 4, 17.1.98

This element of possible failure, (so forcefully illustrated by John Holt in his first book), is irrelevant to the learning for its own sake which most of the families of those interviewed had tried to encourage. With its removal go the psychological blocks against adventurous thinking induced by fear of failure, allowing curiosity and imagination to play a larger part in home-based education than is customary in school. The answers to the following questions show some of the ways in which these faculties, crucial to a sustaining and fulfilling life in a rapidly changing world, developed, and how constantly evolving programmes of individual learning - the word 'programme' being very loosely interpreted - were able to nurture them.

How did you and your family put together a programme?

There are two intriguing aspects to this question. First, where, in the absence of a school curriculum, did the content of what people learnt come from?   Secondly, what helpful innovations emerge from the medley of approaches to learning?

Anthropology versus Wombles

Newly freed from being told what to learn, or never having experienced it, home educated children tended to follow the same path: the one dictated by their interests of the moment and their stage of maturity.

"At school I remember them making me read things like, 'The Wombles', and when I left school I remember just reading things about tribes. We did always have stacks of books."

Harriet

"Dad wanted to cultivate things I personally wanted to do rather than impose things on me - he tried to keep it well rounded but anything I showed a particular interest in I could focus on. It was very much English and art."   Olivia

Edward Proctor gave an example of something that sparked his curiosity, describing a process which is in direct contradiction of normal school methods but appears to have done the trick for his self-motivation:

"I found some books in the library on advanced mathematics. Didn't understand it but I could see it was exciting. The square root of minus one: when I read about this I thought 'This cannot exist!'. That gives you the impetus to go and do something about it, to go and start looking in the more elementary areas and filling in the gaps. I think if it had been organised step-by-step I might have been very bored."

Some children found that the things they were interested in learning about arose out of the activities of daily life, for example as a consequence of their parents having adopted a self-sufficient type of lifestyle into which education could be easily integrated:

> *"I knew the names of every flower and every bird and I knew how to cook and spin and weave."*   Heather

She also emphasises a point made in other studies - that the discrete subject approach so strongly adhered to in the schools tends to fall by the wayside at home, where arbitrary boundaries are redundant:

> *"What I couldn't get my head round about conventional education is the way they try and separate everything into little compartments with subjects called A, B, C and D, whereas I've always found that education is about connecting all the things you know and making a bigger and bigger picture of your knowledge of the world."*

These comments recall those of George and Grace Gordon's mother about school children lacking control, not to mention real understanding, because of never seeing how their bits of learning fit together. They also relate to her children's later experiences at university:

> *"This is something I still can't do. I can't think 'Subjects'."*   George

> *"In home education you're viewing everything as inter-related. One of the reasons I didn't carry on with theology and religious studies at university was because they were refusing to let me use information from one part of it across into another."*   Grace

This seems profoundly anti-educational. One has only to think of some of the great scientific discoveries to appreciate the role of cross-fertilisation in supplying the vital clue that makes the explanation clear. Home educators who do not work to artificial boundaries are training into their children's minds a flexibility which is increasingly valuable in modern employment and self-employment.

A small minority of families took a traditional, subject-based, approach, while still making use of non-school-like opportunities to expand the curriculum:

> *"They tried to teach us a range of normal subjects like geography, geology, English, mathematics. My elder brother did geology, got a BA, and he was setting up his own Field Studies business and used to be around, so he taught us the stuff he knew."*   Charlie

This reflects - as far as one can tell from other studies and from the home education newsletters - a national picture in which a few parents are home educating because they feel they can do the same job as the schools, only better, but most resemble the majority of my interviewees' parents, who want to do a different, non-comparable, job. Paul's parents, who had, as he said earlier, 'reservations' about the school system, copied some of its features without subscribing to others:

> *"It was quite informal really. We set the day aside for maybe three subjects and took it as it came. Obviously it didn't always work out - we'd have arguments. We weren't really bothered about aiming for GCSEs or anything like that."*

A word about literacy. Though their parents varied greatly in the priority they gave it, there was no-one in the study who could not read. The fact that some, for example the Taylor girls, had learnt to do so rather late by school standards, (around nine), did not handicap them academically - both went on to get university degrees, as did Edward, who had learnt at the age of 3:

> *"My grandmother sat down and showed me, like she started me off with the piano, but these things came fairly naturally."*

The school system's emphasis on comparatively early reading seems as arbitrary as its choice of learning matter: after all, they do things differently in many other European countries, with better academic results later on. But once a whole curriculum is geared to the assumption that children will read at a certain age, those who do not will suffer educationally. This suggests that home-based education may have particular advantages for children with dyslexia, or who are emotionally or physically unready to read when the schools decree that they should.

Time, talk and treasure trove

Here I would like to talk about some of the interesting and liberating learning techniques which families beginning to home educate twenty years ago, developed. I will start with those derived from school and then discuss the flexible use of time and children's involvement in organising their days; the role of serendipity in uncovering opportunities for learning; and the benefits of talk.

Some of the families in the study had taken a feature of school ways of working, the 'theme' approach for example, and extended its scope:

> *"We did 'Knights', and we made knight glove puppets and we read knight books, and we went to castles and museums and we did knight history and knight cooking. We even did knight mathematics, I remember."*   Laurence

Another school-like tactic, very much an exception to the general rule among interviewees' families, employed a certain amount of authoritarianism:

> *"You had basic hours when you had to sit down with the books and do the work but once you'd done that, if you wanted to study more you could, but other than that there was quite a lot of freedom."*   Charlie

In this quote and the following one, the amount of time wasted in school is suggested by the reduced hours necessary to cover the same ground at home:

> *"When I was older, academic work averaged a couple of hours a day. The rest of the day was my own to do what I liked with."*   Mandy

Except in Charlie's family, the use of time tended to be radically different from school, in that it was very much a matter for negotiation and the encouragement of individual responsibility:

> *"From when I was about nine Mum used to sit me down at the beginning of the term and say 'Right, what are we going to do this term?' I'd want to be saying 'Nothing'! But I'd think*

about it for a while and then say 'I want to do biology' or whatever. And we'd go out to the bookshop and say 'This looks good'. We'd break that down into weekly goals so we'd say 'Well, if we want to do this book in a year we'd have to do two chapters a week' or something. Then on a Monday morning I'd sit down and say 'Well, if I've got to do that much work this week, I'll do this bit here and this bit here.' That was probably 11, 12 onwards, I would timetable myself. I wouldn't necessarily stick to it but I would say 'On this day I'm going to do these things.'"   Laurence

This is very much the way self-employed adults organise their working week - with outline plans that allow for contingencies. Perhaps this experience was one of the reasons Laurence found himself running his own successful website design business only months after leaving Cambridge. His parents, however, still thought very much in school-like chunks of the calendar, such as terms and weekdays, for academic work. Not all families operated this way, but those that did had the advantage that their children were able to socialise with conventionally educated friends after school, at weekends and in the holidays.

Some degree of flexibility is characteristic of most home educating families - inevitably so, if education is to be part of daily life in the real world, rather than shut off from it as in school:

"It was never terrifically structured - I'd occasionally do a timetable but not really stick to it. Just meandering along. I spent a lot less time actually doing lessons than a lot of other people."   Chloe

One interviewee was slightly equivocal about the benefits of flexibility, but he eventually argued against his original position:

"A disadvantage possibly is the fact that I've not had to do 9 to 3 every day and get into that rhythm. I don't know if it's a **bad** *thing, but it's a bit more difficult for me to get into that whole study thing. I have been to college and I didn't find it much of a problem actually. That was just a year, City and Guilds. It was much more structured than studying at home - I*

didn't find that particularly hard. I quite enjoyed it."   Paul

The issue of serendipity's valuable role in home education runs deeply counter to the prescribed curriculum-bites culture of the school system and crops up again and again in the comments of interviewees.   It suggests that worthwhile learning can come about by chance, increasing lateral thinking ability and enabling someone to make a connection that has previously been elusive, or firing their enthusiasm for an entirely new topic. It relates to the question of crossing subject barriers, already referred to:

> *"I found very often that an apparently unrelated subject suddenly could become important to something else."*
>
> Edward

This raises the importance of exposing children who have a less structured education to all sorts of opportunities for learning, some chosen at random and some not:

> *"I think there's probably quite a big split in the EO movement at the moment between people who sit their five-year-olds down with a very structured curriculum and people who just leave them, saying one day they'll suddenly realise they're interested in quantum mechanics or whatever. You can't be interested in something until you know there's something to be interested in."* Pauline James, mother of Sally and Andrew

Useful ideas and new thinking can come from anywhere:

> *"Some of the best learning will come from problems. We were doing an experiment and it wouldn't work, and we'd say 'Well, why didn't it work?' So rather than doing a pre-ordained thing we'd go off at a tangent - we were doing caterpillars growing into butterflies, and the caterpillars got eaten by maggots from the inside, so it was quite interesting because we aimed to go this way and ended up going that way. It ended up being very much more powerful because it was real and interactive and it was always better than what we were aiming to do. Coincidental learning."*   Laurence

This sort of real experimentation is not often possible in school - on the rare occasions when the expected outcome does not materialise, pressures of time on the curriculum do not allow pupils to 'go off at a tangent'.

Also contrasting with received school wisdom was the implicit emphasis families placed on talk as a means of expanding horizons, extending thinking skills and learning to communicate clearly with a range of people. Mollie Taylor explained two of the benefits of this easy intercourse:

> *"I've never found tutors intimidating. People at university can get very nervous around people they see as authority figures, but when you're at home, because you have conversations with your parents and they're the people you're finding things out from, it's not like school teachers where you'd be more frightened to ask. You don't notice the division in the world so much: you don't notice, 'This is the children's world, and this is the adults' world'."*

Mollie's comment that home educated children may feel more comfortable about asking for information or an explanation of something they do not understand, suggests another reason for their frequently reported academic success. At home the one-to-one situation enables any explanation to be both thorough and tailored exactly to the needs of the enquirer, with which the adult is familiar.

A continual exchange of ideas, feelings and opinions was also the medium by which children influenced the course of their education:

> *"It was a question of me asking and following up things I was interested in. I remember doing a project on spiders and a project on Ancient Egypt: what grabbed my attention as an eight year old. And following my own agenda of spending a lot of time reading."*   Chloe

Other benefits of talk-based learning were summarised in a report on a 1990 M.Phil thesis by a Bristol student, G.F.Clarkson, which appeared in *EO News* :

> *"New knowledge has to be connected with what is known before learning can occur; a process most easily effected by*

talk... Talk stimulates the creation of new thoughts as well as the recall of existing knowledge... An interested audience gives a real purpose for the talk and encourages further reflection about both content and language... Thinking through the spoken word is more effective and quicker than writing the same thoughts, and the difficulty of producing written code may interfere with the thinking process."
Paula Fielding-Bell, *EO News* 124, Oct 1998, p19

The enormous opportunities for learning through conversation which the home educating family can provide are creating a lot of interest amongst the movement's members as a whole and, as we will see in the section on social skills, they make a valuable contribution to self-confidence and articulacy in the wider world.

A final point about the way in which home education programmes evolve is that adults seem to learn as much as their children, through being open to new interests or attitudes to life which children introduce into the family, and through continually developing their understanding of how people learn:

"I've learnt a great deal from my daughter about what it is to be a woman."   Pauline James

"I'd learn as well, through teaching my daughter."   Flora

"It was such a learning process for all three of us - my Dad as well."   Chloe

Because of this growing interest and expertise in how people learn, several of the parents who had not originally been teachers ended up in a paid teaching job, (though none in a school!). Mrs Cassell impressed the LEA to such an extent that they asked her to tutor some of their 'school refusers'. Other parents, such as Pippa Hawkins' mother, went into adult education. This indicates, perhaps, that some of the thinking behind home-based education is beginning in informal ways to influence the orthodox system.

What part did creativity play in your activities?

"They picked people who had their own imagination. You had to write a proposal for a radio script, to send in with your

application."   Heather, commenting on how she came to be accepted for a degree in broadcasting.

"There's no such thing as 'wrong'."   George

These comments reminded me that creativity is not restricted to the art, writing, music or theatre we immediately think of - activity in all these areas has a spin-off affecting the whole mind, influencing performance in traditional academic and technical fields as well as giving people enjoyment and satisfaction in their leisure time or becoming their chosen work. (Andrew James, for example, spent a lot of time as a teenager doing photography, and followed this interest through university to become a TV documentary film producer and director.)

Interviewees had spent more time on what might loosely be called 'artistic' activities than would be possible in school, where creative subjects are increasingly marginalised, partly for financial reasons and partly because they are devalued by a curriculum geared to the economic needs of society. The proportion of interviewees who had seriously pursued some kind of creative endeavour was well over half.

Harriet took to the boards at 12, working with a puppeteer and then going full-time to a local theatre school, demonstrating the advantage of home education for activities which demand dedication. The availability of so much time allows the development of talent to whatever level is possible:

"I had the chance to explore my own creativity. It was a natural thing to spend hours and hours doing something that fascinated me without having to switch off at the end of an hour when the bell rang."   Chloe

The element of choice in most home educating families may prevent children from suffering the parental pressure that often goes with creativity, particularly in the performing arts. There were opportunities to try different creative outlets rather than an expectation of being a shining prodigy in just one, as this recollection of a rather Brontë-like inner world suggests:

"We had a little group of us that met through EO. We did recorders and a bit of story-writing and a lot of drawing. I

*remember playing a lot of imaginative games with my sister,
being quite inventive with whole stories surrounding our
games, the history of them. That's mainly what we did, rather
than having lessons."*   Mollie

Grace's mother explained how Grace tinkered about in several
artistic areas before deciding it was music she wanted to explore
seriously, (leading eventually to grade exams, a degree, and
finally a Ph.D.):

*"When you first started to write, you used to make up stories,
and when you first started to dance, you used to make up
dances. When you started to do music, you wanted to write
pieces of music... She always wanted to be at the creative end
of it."*

This happy pluralism continued throughout her years of home
education, since she continued to dance, and the whole family
became involved in local amateur dramatics.

Because of her own experience of creative freedom, Grace was
able to analyse the reactions of her more conventionally educated
music students to the challenge of composing:

*"They're absolutely terrified! Just taking them through their
first composition: 'What do I do?' 'You can do anything. Isn't
that wonderful?' "*

The value of having developed creative interests as a child which
now provided a source of fulfilment outside work or study was
much appreciated, even when the creative pull was in conflict
with other demands:

*"I still paint, I nearly did it for a degree, so I miss it. It's
another thing you don't always get time to do. You feel like
you **need** to do it sometimes."*   Mollie

*"I've been writing a lot since I was little, so that's another
thing I want to explore if I can find the time. I've just had my
first poem published, which was exciting."*   Chloe

There was one dissenting voice where the effects of imaginative
thinking were concerned. Olivia said that the creative start she
had had at home, which led eventually to a degree in film and

TV, as well as script-writing and guitar-playing in her spare time, had its drawbacks when family circumstances forced her into school:

"I lost a lot of marks, not doing what was expected. In secondary school it's very structured: in geography you all learn about the same things, the same example: 'Write about the Statue of Liberty', or something. I'd be looking for my personal angle to take on it, and I was doing all these fantastic things. Dad was encouraging me and I was getting terrible marks... I hate not having leeway, I hate being pinned down!"

Whether this says more about the possible disadvantages of encouraging creativity in home education or about the limiting of the imagination which may result from strict adherence to the National Curriculum and all its works, I leave to the reader to judge.

Is learning still important to you?

'Lifelong learning', in the sense of re-training for second or even third careers or as a way of keeping the mind alert in old age, has recently become the darling of education ministers and economists alike - but for the last twenty years home educators have recognised that education is a continuous process, without artificial cut-off points at 5, 16 or 21 years, and a process, furthermore, well suited to the ever-changing nature of modern life. Sally James related her typical point of view to her own and her daughter's experience in and out of school:

"I'm learning all the time. I don't like the structure in schools because I think kids constantly learn, on so many levels. You can't say, 'Right, you're learning now!' The idea of 'free time' is part of the same thing. It's completely unnatural. "

The people I interviewed were, without exception, still interested in learning, all undertaking some sort of formal or informal education, and convinced that, in George's words: *"The day I stop learning'll be the day I die."*

The difference between this attitude and that of some conventionally educated people, who regard learning as a means to an end rather than worth doing for its own sake, was illustrated by his sister Grace's comments:

> *"Some of the first year students said to me 'What are you going to do when you've finished your Ph.D? Is it going to make any difference?' I said 'Well, I'll still be interested, I'll still carry on looking at things.'"*

Andrew, the film-maker, commented, *"We never stop learning"*, but added that keeping body and soul together tended to be a bigger priority for most people. He saw a need for the widening of educational opportunities and, inevitably perhaps, from his special perspective, thought television had a big role to play in this.

Those interviewees who educated themselves because of bad experiences at school emphasised that it was the setting, not learning itself, that was the problem, and described the attitude that drove them to work hard even where family support was not forthcoming:

> *"I wasn't turned off education at all - it was just the school. I never stopped - every day I would get up and work school hours because I was really keen not to let my mind go to sleep."*   Kate

> *"I learnt to enjoy the learning for learning's sake rather than because it was going to earn me lots of money or get me to university. And to follow threads of my own interests - and not worry about covering everything, because once you've learnt to learn, that's all you need."*   Emma

There was lots of evidence that sparks of interest lit during home education days burst into flames in adulthood: some I have already discussed in the section on creativity. Edward described how his self-taught nature illustration got him the perfect job at Oxford's University Museum, despite a complete lack of academic qualifications:

> *"They were looking for a combination of artistry and entomology. Travelling round museums, I'd sat and drawn. I did a lot of photographic work and I'd done the entomology as*

well. I hadn't got the drawings any more so I dashed out, bought some paper and paints and inks and worked solidly for the weekend, got these things in the post, went up for interview and they said, 'We'd love to have you!'"

Many of the interviewees had signed up for higher education, sometimes despite severe obstacles:

"Four years ago I started doing a degree with the OU, mainly music and psychology. I haven't been to tutorials because when I started doing it I was more agoraphobic than I am now, and the last course I did, one on learning disability and one on Beethoven, the tutorials were in Birmingham, which was too far away."   Emma

Those who had the opportunity to further their education through work, tackled the challenge with zest, sometimes surprising themselves:

"Having said, 'Thank God, no more exams ever again!' I'm actually studying for several at the moment through Microsoft and Southwestern. It makes sense financially for the company because we get cheaper deals. I'm reading more books than I was at university! If you're in IT then it has to be lifelong learning."   Laurence

"I went on a water project in the Ixil Triangle, which is in a fairly remote area of Guatemala, and lived in the village, had to learn Spanish, they don't speak any English. I tried to learn it in Spain and failed miserably, years before. But there, because they don't speak any other language, I had to speak it. And my grasp of technical Spanish for putting in gravity-fed water systems is unsurpassable! "   Daniel

For others, interests arose in the course of daily life, through being open to new experiences:

"I decided I wanted to learn acrobatics and did a bit of that in London, then when I came to Bristol I did a one-year course called 'Fool Time', which was at the circus school. I've been working in a performance group, doing trapeze. I also did a three-year counselling course and now I have to see a number of supervised clients at the centre to finish the course properly."   Sally

"At the minute I'm a builder's labourer. My partner had a bad bike accident last year and he's paralysed from the chest down. The house had to be totally rebuilt so I've been helping out there. It's good fun, I'm learning lots of new things again."   Mandy

Mollie suddenly realised that she was interested in learning languages, through being in a similar situation to Daniel:

"It's something that I never thought about until I suddenly needed to speak another one. I needed to communicate."

These examples demonstrate that it is never too late to start learning a language, as some primary educationalists would have us believe, and, furthermore, that having a practical incentive to do so may be more than half the battle. The same thing applies to music, as Kate, who did not start playing the cello until her mid-teens and ended up studying it at Oxford, suggested. (There is an excellent book by John Holt, *Never too Late*, on this theme.)

Spontaneous Combustion

This chapter's title, *Lighting a fire*, refers not only to the passion for a particular intellectual, creative, sporting or technical pursuit that may be ignited by deliberate or chance exposure in the course of home education, but also to the general enthusiasm for learning which interviewees applied to anything they came across: spontaneous combustion, if that's not straining the metaphor too much. Daniel explained his theory about why they maintained their curiosity and determination, a theory based on a view of human nature that most readers will accept as fundamentally, if puzzlingly, true:

"There's few things I'm not interested in - because there wasn't anyone standing behind me saying, 'You've got to read this book because it's education'. If you'd have picked up 'Jane Eyre' as a leisure read, you'd have really enjoyed it. If somebody says, 'You've got to read this eight times and we're going to be asking questions', you'd do anything, anything, rather than have to read it. Because I was able to read an awful lot around a lot of subjects, I was able to find a lot to interest me."

Chloe agreed, and supplies the last word on the role of home education in promoting lifelong learning:

> *"That's stayed with me - I am very interested in things. I felt when I went to sixth form that my fellow students were going 'God! You're really interested in this, aren't you?' They were quite jaded by then because they'd been put through it for years. I'd had a different way of learning. If you were learning about some craft thing from someone who actually made a living at it or having French lessons off a local Frenchwoman, it was more of a living experience. I don't really like to compare but that's how it worked for me: it kept things more alive."*

Chapter three

As much possibility as possible

*"The important thing as parents is to give your child as much
exposure to as much opportunity, as much possibility, as
possible, to allow them to evolve the choice themselves."*
                                                            Daniel

This comment, with its echo of the preceding chapter's discussion
about introducing children to the world and letting them select the
bits that interest them, raises two questions: where do you find
resources, including teachers, (in the broad sense of people to
learn from), and how do you afford them? Thirdly, if you choose
to slot in to formal education at any point, have you got the
intellectual tools to make good use of the resources available?

How did you find teachers that suited you?

Many children had learnt a lot from their parents:

*"My parents were very good teachers. They were devoted,
interested. Anything I wanted to do they'd help me research."*
                                                            Olivia

Specific talents, not always along traditional academic lines, were
exploited wherever possible:

*"Mum basically taught us English and maths and she's half-
French so she taught us that as well. My Dad used to take a
couple of afternoons off and he used to teach us the sciences,
chemistry and stuff."*   Paul

*"My father retired when I was twelve - he was a very practical
sort of chap, and used to go round doing lots of things, so it
gave me a sort of polymath approach. And Dad was a big
arguer, he was an argumentative old git and he was always
taking contrary views and arguing devil's advocate. It did*

make me take accepted thoughts and say, 'Is this necessarily the way things are?'"   Daniel

As the people with primary responsibility for their children's education, parents were often the main educators in the very early years but, as George explained, and as critics of home education sometimes suggest, children outgrow their expertise:

> *"Because we were unstructured in the way we were doing things, you very, very rapidly became the expert. It might only be an infinitesimally tiny bit but you've just read it; the other person hasn't. Therefore if you're in advance of the person that's guiding you, they've always got to catch up. They can't tell you where the branches are: you have to find them and decide on which branch to take."*

Far from being a problem, this was seen as a valuable opportunity for children to begin to direct their own learning, find resources other than those their parents could provide, and develop self-discipline, initiative and independence of thought - the very qualities which uninformed people often predict will be lacking when home educated children grow up - the 'apron strings' scenario.

Most interviewees also felt that it was important for parents and children to have time away from each other, as it is for perhaps the majority of people in close relationships:

> *"I did like having time out from my Mum. Having one teacher all to yourself gets a bit much."*   Harriet

Nearly all the families appreciated the many advantages of working with appropriate and stimulating mentors outside the home who suited a particular individual's learning style, and found ways for their children to achieve this. Sometimes other family members with particular interests were drafted in, such as Charlie's brother and Edward's gran. More often, adults with a particular skill, such as Harriet's puppeteer colleague, were pleased to pass it on to a fellow enthusiast:

> *"We had a good artist as a teacher, and photography. I did enjoy it."*   Harriet

"I had a Steiner teacher my Mum knew who gave me maths lessons for a while - basically friends of my parents who had various skills, like somebody did crafts with me."   Chloe

"Mum had a friend who was an art tutor, so we went to him for one half day a week. And I had guitar lessons." Paul

Visitors to the house were also valuable sources of education: Pauline described the impact of their many international guests, such as the South African refugee who turned up on their doorstep at seven in the morning. Other families had similarly interesting short or long term visitors, of which more in the next chapter. The two girls whose parents were not involved much in their home education found their own teachers:

"I made contact with the biology teacher at school and got him to write me a list of all the essays he was going to give my friends, and I asked if he'd mark them and he said he would, so I used to send three essays a week with my friend." Emma

How did you keep costs within the family budget?

Kate found a tutor who had to be paid for - this question of possible expense is another one which often bothers prospective home educators and leads opponents to state that home education is only feasible in comfortably-off families. Grace subscribed to this view:

"There's always been people who haven't got the confidence - but because you're all having to pay for schools anyway, there's going to be a lot of people who really couldn't for financial reasons, because Social Security won't say teaching your own children is a good enough reason not to be looking for a job."

Karen Gold's father, writing in *EO News* in 1989, talked about the cost to his family in those days:

"Financially, a question rarely discussed in these columns, books, videos, tapes in lieu of school will have cost us about £100 this year. In terms of working at home instead of for others, I will have lost about £160 per week, net: that's including the cost of baby-sitters / home heating / take away meals."

Nowadays it is easier than it was to swap, rather than pay for, skills, because of the more extensive networks of home educators: e.g. *"Charlotte has had art lessons with another EO mother who is an artist, in exchange for me teaching her daughter English."*

EO News 124, p8

My interviewing experience, as well as personal friendships in the movement and the continuing lack of comments on economic aspects in *EO News*, suggest that it is rare for financial considerations to be the deciding factor in whether or not to educate at home. Only one interviewee gave me an example of this:

"I was sent to school when I was 10 or 11 because my parents both got jobs - Dad was intending to take me out again, till maybe the age of sixteen, but I never went back out." Olivia

How, then, did the other families manage to earn enough to live on and home educate at the same time? There was a huge variety of solutions. Some were straightforwardly traditional, with one parent, not necessarily the father, (see Karen Gold's family, above), in full-time work and one parent at home with the children:

*"I was always around. I didn't do a great deal with them but I was there if needed. I watched a lot of the schools programmes with them so that I could follow it up afterwards. The only thing I did to earn money was home tuition. I had them in our home so I was still there. It was very good for these children I taught to see there were children out of school **not** because they'd been naughty or truanting or having difficulties. Occasionally, according to the child, we did things together."* Pauline

In a couple of cases, for example Charlie's, where he and his brothers and sisters were adopted by Mr and Mrs Curtis after they had already brought up their natural family, parents had retired and chose to devote their time to home-based education.

In Kate's single parent family, her drive to learn provided the motivation for her to take responsibility for her own education while her mother was out at work - as a teenager she was well able to look after herself during the day. Another single parent family, Sally's second generation home educating one, had adopted the increasingly common mixture of part-time paid and voluntary occupations which enables many home educating families, and indeed other so-called 'downshifters', who are not fussed about a high material standard of living, to juggle the needs of children, parents and the budget and put a higher value on time as a resource. (More about this in chapter 5.)

This way of life was often found in self-employed families, like the Woods, who had a candle-making business, or the Taylors: one parent could be working and the other doing something with the child, or if the child were happily occupied at home or elsewhere, both parents could give their attention to the business.

> *"They've been quite radical. They helped set up 'Education Otherwise' in the first place. Neither of them were teachers - they were trying to be self-sufficient. They'd left good jobs where we lived before and wanted to do something more down to earth, so we moved to the country."*   Heather

These multifarious arrangements are typical of the 'where there's a will, there's a way' approach which families apply to all the economic aspects of home education: setting careful priorities and exercising ingenuity seem to be its hallmarks. Co-operative buying schemes are a useful idea:

> *"They used to get all the stationery through a consortium, a local run thing where you could get all the textbooks and pencils and things cheaper."*   Flora

Contemporary home educators are applying this principle to other areas, and using bulk food-buying schemes to liberate money for educational resources or just to survive. They also have the advantage of free admission to many museums and attractions which give this privilege to school parties.

The parents in the study usually had lots of books already, and either bought, new or second-hand, or borrowed, a lot more, as the occasion demanded. Nowadays, it is increasingly possible to get loans from development centres and teacher training libraries, and extra quantities of books from the public libraries - how long this situation will persist, with the frequent budget cuts these institutions suffer, is a moot point. Edward, from a rather book-less background, exploited the libraries energetically in the course of his peripatetic self-education:

> *"I had a bit of pocket money - that was spent on books, and at that time there was a very good Boots circulating library. You couldn't normally get advanced works there but you could get books and have them for a certain length of time. You could collect them in one town, read them, and hand them in in another town. It was a wonderful system, and you could always go down to reference libraries in the larger cities and use those facilities, and so I always had a vague sort of thing in my mind that I knew where to look things up."*

Access to the Internet and huge works such as encyclopaedia on CD-ROM, have changed the research opportunities for home educators, both at home and in libraries and places like Cyber-cafes and community centres, out of all recognition since my interviewees' childhood. Few of the older ones used computers at all, so their cost was not an issue, but for some of the younger ones, Laurence for instance, computers played an increasingly important part in their education and constituted an extra item to be added to the budget. Television programmes, such as the schools ones mentioned by Pauline, were used by many home educating families, at minimal cost - and radio, of course, is free.

Activities such as sport and drama sometimes present a challenge to home educators, but even isolated families, like the Curtises, were able to overcome the difficulties:

> *"I went with my gran to join the Christmas choir and the plays that she did with her drama society. I was mostly into athletics because we lived in a forest which was pretty good for running."*   Charlie

> *"I got to know a lot of people from the local Steiner school - the one I went to for two days - I got to know the whole class that I would have been in. I used to play cricket for them and go to all the sports days."*   Paul

Science resources are often put forward as impossible to provide at home. Not so: there are ways round every problem of this sort, sometimes very exciting ones!

"Dad trained as a scientist at university and he was highly enthusiastic about doing science in the home. He'd have little laboratories made up wherever we lived and I can remember when I was about four or five, he said, 'To-day dear, we're going to make oxygen.' He took me down into the cellar, with all these pipes and tubes everywhere, and said, 'Everything's fine unless this tube gets blocked'. It got blocked and blew the cellar up! Dad said, 'Never turn your back on an experiment. We'll go and do it again.' We went down and blew it up again! We worked it all out in the end, why the pipe had got blocked. And we always made fireworks for Bonfire Night, ground up the gunpowder and everything."

Mandy

For those who liked to live less dangerously, there were more conventional, but perhaps also more expensive, solutions:

"For the practical side of science we had a lot of do-it-yourself bits of paper and sticky-backed plastic and a lot of science kits: every Christmas and birthday we'd get science kits. But things like chemistry get harder: as you get older there's less you can do at home because there's more equipment needed. When I was 14 I started going to the sixth-form college part-time and the two subjects I was going to do were GCSE electronics and chemistry."   Laurence

This neatly introduces the subject of the next discussion: the use of institutional education as a resource which supplements other activities, or as a way of achieving specific goals.

How did you make use of formal educational opportunities, if at all?

The flexible approach to finding resources adopted by the families in the study included a willingness to use whatever elements of the formal educational system seemed appropriate to a child's needs and compatible with the rest of his or her learning - having their cake and eating it, and why not? Their taxes had paid for it after all, as Grace pointed out, and in many ways this mix of home-based and learning centre-based education, used flexibly according to family circumstance and need, seems a good way forward to a future that could include parents who currently lack the confidence to take greater responsibility for their children's education. (See John Adcock's *In Place of Schools* and Roland Meighan's *The Next Learning System* for more detailed discussion about this.)

There were three ways in which families used the resources of the formal educational world: as a correspondence course for exam purposes, as a part-time top-up to home education or as a full-time option at a stage when children and parents felt this would be beneficial for some reason.

Horses for courses

Correspondence courses were not widely used, possibly because they tend to be costly, as one of the interviewees who had tried them discovered:

> "I did correspondence courses in general science and English - it was down to me to be dedicated enough to study them. They were expensive, so eventually the money ran out and we just bought textbooks and I went through them myself." Kate

The textbook-and-syllabus route was a more common one for teenagers doing GCSEs at home; cheaper, but more demanding in terms of self-discipline and independent thinking because of the lack of feedback from a tutor.

Many, in fact most, interviewees opted for the sixth-form college exam machine at some point and were able to fit it in with their home-based activities through negotiation with the administrators if this was what they wanted to do. Note that the way the subjects were chosen - according to the interviewee's abilities and interests at the time - is very different from the school approach of getting a large number of GCSEs out of the way at once, and then going on to A levels:

> "I did maths O level and maths O/A at home, the chemistry and electronics at college and biology and environmental

*studies at home. Then the next year, when I was 15/16 I did A
level maths and French GCSE at home, but partly with a
French tutor. And then English and economics GCSE at the
college and I started doing chemistry A level there that year.
It was four mornings at college and one day and four
afternoons at home. Then the next year was about 50/50. The
college was very supportive - I'd passed the entry
requirements and they could do part-time and they could get
the funding - they were amazingly helpful."*   Laurence

Laurence went on to point out that by the time his brother wanted
to do a similar thing the college regulations had changed and he
was having to pay for it:

*"It seems ironic that they'll either pay £20,000 for your
education or they'll **charge** you if you only have a little bit!"*

Interpretations of the rules vary from time to time and from place
to place, and with flexi-colleging as with flexi-schooling, where
children spend part of their time in school and part at home,
interviewees found that an individual approach to the principal
was the best tactic to adopt.

Those few who started school full-time before the sixth-form stage
mostly went to Steiner schools, whose philosophy tends to sit
better with the emphasis on child-centred learning in home-based
education than does that of the orthodox system. They were
regarded as a useful transitional resource, as Heather, who
attended the local Steiner school after 6 years of home education
and then had another year out before sixth-form college,
commented:

*"I think it was a good stepping-stone. I think I would have found
it harder if I'd gone to a normal school because I think the school
you go to at eleven, that's quite a bad time for a lot of people but
I'd sort of got my confidence up by going to the Steiner school."*

Pippa had a couple of years at a Steiner school before going to the
local High School to do GCSEs:

*"It was there as an option and we went along to try it.   It
provided the social side of things but it was less formal than the
state schools. That was a good experience as well - provided
another range of activities to do."*

Dropping into the system full-time at the sixth-form stage, for the sausage-machine reasons referred to above, some people were concerned about whether they would be as well equipped to operate it as those who had been completely institutionalised from five years old:

> "I was worried about it because there's quite a mystique around exams. If you're taught at home the thing that's always thrown up at you is, 'Well, you're never going to get any exams!' So you get used to this thing that you're never going to get any exams. And then you find that actually it's just writing what you know on a piece of paper, either in the right way or the wrong way. One of the big differences was that I was there because I chose to be but a lot of the people doing GCSEs were there because their parents said they had to go back and get some exams - and because they'd failed once their confidence was affected."   Heather

Several interviewees stressed this point about the importance of motivation, and of already being in the habit of disciplining yourself to work:

> "The thing I found really good, which made a big difference, was whereas everybody else was sick of working in that way, I was always able to, and still am, structure my time, and I'm doing it because I want to do it and I don't need anyone to tell me that this is what you need to do."   Pippa

Kate felt she appreciated the range of resources in her sixth form more than her fellow students did, because there had been a dearth of them at home:

> "You had all these computers and books and you could play around with things. When people had been at school all that time they were so accustomed to it, it was boring, but I enjoyed it."

As far as being academically up to the mark on their entry to the classroom, interviewees reported no problems, in fact mostly the reverse:

> "At college you'd have to go through example after example after example - you have to wait until everyone's caught up,

obviously. It usually meant I'd done my homework before, in
class. I'd have got ahead,"   Laurence

Some were critical of a lack of academic rigour, particularly at the
higher education level, where an annoying lack of organisation
led to less-than-stimulating experiences:

"It's so lax I'm only in two days a week. You can get away
with filming anything, so long as you can justify it, completely
blag your way through it. Sometimes it's very tense - because
it's badly organised so sometimes you have three massive
essays to do all at once, sometimes you've got nothing at all.
There's a couple of very good tutors but they can't do
anything about it - nothing ever changes. This is my third
year and we noticed in the first year how air-headed some of
the tutors seemed to be, not knowing particularly what they
were supposed to be doing."   Olivia

"It was one of the biggest disappointments in my life, going to
university: it was awful. For a communications department
they were the most disorganised people that I've come
across."   Heather

Higher education can be as much of a lottery as compulsory age
schooling, as the contrasting comments of Heather's sister Mollie
bear out:

"Have you heard of ERASMUS exchanges? I'm going to
Spain with that, as part of the course, but because I'm doing
Latin American studies I get a year in South or Central
America as part the research for my dissertation. It's such a
good course, I can't believe more people don't do it."

A mismatch between teaching and learning styles, not to mention
expectations, was sometimes a problem, (and I apologise for both
examples being about Cambridge - it may or may not be
significant):

"The way science is at Cambridge, they'd write everything on
the board and you'd copy it down. It was disastrous because
they're not actually talking to you about anything. If you'd
been through school you were OK because over the years
you'd got this skill that I never had."   Jim

"It was very theoretical. The stuff I'd done at home, and the later practical stuff, I was used to everything having a reason. I made the decision in my first year to hope for a First but academically it wasn't going to be my biggest thing, my only thing, and to make the most of Cambridge. It seemed to me that to get a First you had to take aboard so much useless knowledge. I think exams at Cambridge are the worst - they're not testing you as an engineer, they're testing you as an exam taker. Doing well in exams is very different to doing well as an engineer."   Laurence

On the other hand, some interviewees with experience of a range of teaching styles found themselves in a position to interpret for their fellow students:

"I ended up virtually as a translator. The teacher would explain it one way and I'd explain it to the person sitting next to me in a completely different way, that they understood."
                                                              Grace

The importance of matching the resource to the individual's needs and aptitudes is perhaps the thread that runs through this chapter - but the vastness of possibilities in the real world, once families stop thinking in terms of purely school-type facilities, ensures that, with ingenuity and imagination, these can be met in a way that caters for all learning styles and all interests. Two aspects in particular of real world experience available to people being educated from a home base - travel and work - will be investigated in the next two chapters, the first in the context of developing empathy and social understanding, and the second in terms of finding some kind of fulfilling working role in life.

Chapter four

Sort of nerdy with an anorak?

"It could go badly wrong: I can anticipate you'd come out at the age of 17 or 18 all sort of nerdy with an anorak, or dressed in your Mum's clothes!"　　　　Daniel

This comment perhaps expresses some of the worst fears of parents contemplating home-based education - it is also a regular objection voiced by members of the public. I have to report that none of my interviewees was clothed in any way unusually, although I can't vouch for those I spoke to on the phone!

Social development

Arguments against the social environment of school as preparation for adult life have been well made elsewhere, by John Holt (*Teach your Own*), Roland Meighan (*Theory and Practice of Regressive Education*) and Chris Shute (*Compulsory Schooling Disease*), among others. Bullying by pupils and teachers; restricted social expectations imposed by age-limited classrooms; and the artificiality of social intercourse dictated by school regulations, have been thoroughly examined.

From the point of view of educating children to interact with older people or, in time, their own children, the school sets up a poor model of adult/child relationships. Its imposed authority may not distinguish much between major and minor infringements of rules, and the use of negotiation based on mutual respect may be limited. This has not proved a happy way to run a community, nor, despite all the current talk of education for citizenship, does it offer practical experience of the democratic values children will encounter on leaving.

Olivia gave her analysis of the relationships she encountered at school:

> *"I expected to be treated with respect by the teachers. I didn't understand the relationship, getting told off. I was speaking to the teacher as another person rather than as God. I only respected two or three teachers: if they seemed to enjoy what they were doing, if they were human and communicated with pupils as people rather than annoying brats."*

Home educating families, working on a small scale, are ideally placed to use the strategies of negotiation and consideration of each member's views in a way that prepares children to be flexible and empathetic but able to argue for their own needs. Informal social education at home can focus on quality rather than quantity: not how many birthday parties youngsters are invited to, to take a trivial example, but whether the friendships they have enable them to know themselves better and learn to live well with others, (as well as having fun of course!). The word 'socialisation' has too many connotations of moulding a person to behave in prescribed, not to say proscribed, ways for me to be comfortable using it: 'social education', seems to do the job rather better.

Emotional development

On a psychological level this entails beginning to understand their emotional strengths and weaknesses and use them constructively in relationships and learning. Sally suggested how adults could help, and how the ethos prevalent in conventional educational settings tended to hinder:

> *"Through doing counselling I believe it's really important that kids express their emotions: if they're upset they cry and 'get over it better. People working with small children are taught to distract: they're upset, show them something else and they forget. They don't really forget. It comes back later. I'm helping my kids to talk about things that upset them. Boys are really vulnerable: at such an early age they're taught to suppress their feelings."*

Turning from awareness of their own emotions to the equally important understanding of what others might be thinking or feeling, Laurence's mother explained how reading with her children extended their capacity for empathy:

"I try to practise the widely held EO philosophy of learning by doing but I don't want my kids to have to go through a war, be a refugee or face their parents' divorce. However I would like them to have some understanding of these situations. Fiction can bring feelings into places, bring people alive."

EO News

The Taylor girls' mother felt that security enabled children to react to others in an emotionally constructive way:

"If the child is provided with a stable and loving environment when small and not prematurely forced from it, he or she will not need to react aggressively to other children or find security in doing something better than someone else."

EO News

A final aspect of this discussion of emotional development in education is its huge effect on learning, something which many people have appreciated intuitively but which has only recently become the subject of serious research:

"..remarkably little attention seems to be given to the impact of pupils' psychological state on their capacity to learn...what makes one child a keen and successful student and another passive and relatively less-successful has at least as much to do with that pupil's emotional intelligence as it does with more well-recognised intellectual abilities. Each of us could produce an anecdote about an individual judged to be a failure at school who later revealed unrecognised talents."

Patricia Broadfoot, *Times Educational Supp*, 6.11.98

Daniel Goleman's book, *Emotional Intelligence*, describes how emotional states affect ability to learn. He also discusses the ways in which Howard Gardner's concept of 'Multiple Intelligences' can be used to make education appropriate to the individual, (whether his or her talent is a traditionally valued academic one or not), thereby reducing fear and boredom and increasing commitment to learning and enjoyment of new challenges.

This chapter examines how the encouragement of social and emotional awareness can flourish in home educating families, looking at how social contacts arise when they are not enforced by classroom proximity and what activities promote home education friendships; how other people react to home educated children; and what sort of social lives the interviewees have as adults.

Did the social life of school play a role in your being home educated?

Seven of the interviewees, (the Frampton sisters, Kate, Emma, Jim, Sally and Andrew), left school because the social environment was preventing them from learning, mostly due to fear. Some were consequently less than gregarious:

> "It was hell at the time for me - and I've always been quite shy, so when I did come out I didn't push for a social life."
>
> Flora

> "That school was a disaster for Andrew - he had no idea of the culture. All you learned was to get away with as little as possible. He was bullied. When he came out of school he spent hours watching old films. It was what he needed - the only way of healing his damaged psyche."   Pauline

Kate, on the other hand, missed her school friends, (whom she might have lost touch with anyway, because they went to a different secondary school). She was the only interviewee who felt her social life suffered through home education and, significantly, one of three who got little family support, which probably increased her loneliness:

> "My social life at home was poor - I kept in touch with people from primary school but it was difficult because our lives were so different. They had other friends and a different social life. I did things like tennis and swimming but I didn't have that closeness you get at school. Once I went back and made good friends I realised what I'd been missing." She adds, "I didn't feel out of my depth socially, though."

It's interesting to note that Kate's story refutes the theory that 'phobics' should be forced back into school or they will never be able to face up to life's challenges. Her voluntary re-entry to the system after spending most of her secondary years at home proved less difficult than she feared:

> *"I went back when I was 17, into a different school. I was thinking about my future and I wanted to study music. I felt this was my last chance to get some qualifications. I thought 'I've just got to do this', so I made myself go. It was hard at first but then I started doing well and loving it."*

Her happiness and success illustrate the potential value of a flexible system, in which it would be common and acceptable for time out of school and time in school to be taken when the individual felt each was appropriate. Sally also appreciated the value of such a break during her teenage years:

> *"I was not capable of making relationships at that age - having the time out probably did help to get myself sorted."*

How did you find a social life while you were home educated?

If we accept, as anthropology suggests, that human beings, with rare exceptions, have a natural need to associate with other human beings for much of the time and for a variety of purposes, we can assume that for those interviewees who had not been emotionally damaged by school, the company of others was important. (The rare exception here was Edward, who relished time on his own, a reaction perhaps to the frenetic show business world.)

How, then, did the normally sociable majority find like-minded people to pursue activities with, and the close friends which most people value greatly as adding balance and enjoyment to life? An obvious starting point was an already existing interest, as Harriet explained:

> *"Mum didn't drive, it was a small village and I needed people around me. If I don't like something I'll change it. I threw myself into a group thing, the theatre. I've always lived with a lot of people whereas Flora seemed quite on her own. You*

don't have to be isolated. It depends on your personality, whether you've got the confidence to go out and meet people."

Despite Harriet's perception of her sister's isolation, Flora appears to have found social activities that suited her:

"I had penfriends from EO and they used to visit. I went on holiday once a year, with a huge girl-group. I had my own social life but nothing to do with local things apart from the friends I already had - there were other groups that I went to, the arts more often."

Laurence seems to have had a go at almost everything, and prefaces his remarks with a comment about the time available for socialising in school:

"I didn't feel I was missing out because at school you just have breaks and lunchtime together. I used to play in the street with the kids: at school you finish at 3.30 so most of your life spent with people is not during school. I used to go to Cubs, Scouts. I did St. John's Ambulance for years, and Drama Club, Outdoor Club, gymnastics, swimming, EO weekends."

Emma explained how clubs were easier for her than school:

"My big thing was, 'At school I'm trapped. I can't get home when I want to.' With clubs I could leave when I felt like it, so I went to Brownies and things and went out with friends."

With the lack of homework in the evenings, home educated people are in a better position to make relaxed use of the huge variety of clubs and classes available than school children who have to fit them into a busy schedule. Some families were lucky enough to live in friendly places with a ready-made social life, where there was no prejudice against them because of their rejection of school:

"I used to go around with friends in the village. When I was about 6 or 7 I went along to Sunday School. I'm not religious but I thought it was a good way of meeting people. Because there wasn't many kids in the village you got to know them all and play with them. The grown-ups were great, they were all

friendly. I used to go and see some of the little old ladies, do a bit of shopping for them." Mandy

Mandy's mention of 'little old ladies' introduces one of the valuable aspects of the community-based social life which home educators seek to provide: the opportunity to mix with a wide age range for much of the time, and learn to empathise with people of different circumstances and outlooks. Sometimes this came about through a shared interest:

"Both children had easy relationships with adults, which a lot of children that age wouldn't have had. We knew a Kodak scholar who was a student at the Polytechnic of Central London, doing photography, very gifted, and Andrew worked with him. And we met a woman photographer who made a name for herself, and he worked with her." Pauline

(These comments recall the section in the previous chapter on finding appropriate teachers - so often this kind of mentoring relationship, based on a particular interest, bears no resemblance to teacher/student relationships in school.)

Family activities sometimes provided the opportunity to meet people with different perspectives:

"There was someone who helped Dad in the pottery - he lived with us, and then his girl-friend did as well. We did a lot of fairs, which was a big part of growing up. There was always a lot of other adults and children around - a wide set of people. That had an influence on me wanting to travel. I love meeting people." Mollie

Mollie's mention of travel suggests another potent source of extended social horizons. In my study it was older teenagers who went travelling independently, but there are reports from America of 16 year-olds going off on extensive cycling trips. (See the book by Grace Llewellyn.)

What social benefits did my interviewees feel they gained from their adventures? Edward described some of his experiences with the circus:

"You saw so many different things. You were living with different people all the time. Years ago, people didn't mix

*much with people from other countries, other backgrounds,
but I always had that. We worked for six months in Spain,
1947, and it was an interesting time to be there, they hadn't
recovered from the Civil War. Those cities were what I
imagine Calcutta to be: there were bodies in the streets; the
poverty was incredible."*

From the point of view of increasing social and emotional
awareness through mind-blowing experiences, Edward's travels
resembled those of Mollie and Daniel in South America:

*"Ecuador's amazing. I went when I was 18: I finished my A
levels and worked, to save up, doing credit-card sales, quite
single-mindedly. It's easy to find work there - language
schools are always looking for native speakers. We spent one
month in the jungle teaching English to guides. I felt funny
about it because of being scared of changing the culture. It
was a very intense experience: because we stayed with a
shaman I imagined it would be all spiritual enlightenment. It
was, but in a different way: very tough, very down to earth.
We spent a lot of time going, 'Oh God, I want to get back to
the city!' - because of all the insects biting. I was ill
afterwards, vomiting blood when I came back to Quito - and
Natalie,* (her travelling companion and fellow EOer - Chloe
Cassell's sister), *was ill while we were there. But it's beautiful
and I'm happy that I've seen the forest before it disappears."*

Daniel's experience of voluntary work in Guatemala, apart from
nearly killing him through blood poisoning, added dramatically to
his emotional education, giving him a new perspective on aid.

*"I am very cynical about development work. Not the people -
the majority of field workers are brilliant. But the impact of
what they do is under-considered. One of the biggest risks to
life and limb, in the middle of the jungle, is being run over by
an aid agency truck. I worked in this village of 105 people
and in two weeks two kids died. One was four and the other
thirteen. If those people had been given ten quid to take them
to the hospital and be given drugs, they wouldn't have died of
something stupid like diarrhoea. It's easy to say, 'They're
used to a high mortality rate.' If you're a mother and your
kid dies, it doesn't matter whether you're in bloody Swindon
or some South American country, the kid's just died."*

Travel in the developed world was not as much of a life-shaking event. Chloe had been a *Camp America* volunteer and then stayed on to travel around. Laurence had spent a vacation in the States selling study guides:

> *"I met a lot of home schoolers and it was good to be able to say, 'I was home educated too'. Half of them didn't believe me - thought it was a salesman's pitch."*

Several of my interviewees were planning new travels, demonstrating that the desire to meet people, and curiosity about different ways of life, were still very much alive - a reminder that social and emotional education, like the stimulation of the intellect, need never stop. Kate talked about what she planned to do after completing her music degree:

> *"I won't stay in Oxford for my nursing training - I'll apply somewhere else to do my diploma. I like to travel and see places. After I'm trained I'm going to apply to join the Red Cross."*

Paul had just returned from a visit to 36 cousins in South Africa and was saving for his next adventure:

> *"I'm going travelling this summer, a bit of interrailing - I want to do the eastern part of Europe, which will be quite interesting - also cheap!"*

He had a peripatetic childhood because his psychiatrist father did a lot of locums, but thought this a positive thing - perhaps it increased his appetite for travel. Maybe the family closeness engendered by home-based education is responsible for an emotional security which overrides the unsettled feelings reported by some people who moved around a lot as children. It may also be that family crises are coped with better emotionally because of the extra time available for talking.

If you went to school or college later, how did you fit in socially?

Overwhelmingly, as we have seen, interviewees joined or re-joined the system to make use of facilities for qualifications. The majority of those who went to school, (mostly Steiner), earlier, did not encounter social problems, presumably because they had been used to interacting with a variety of people:

"I fitted in the classes and didn't have any trouble. The same with friends - it wasn't a problem."   **Pippa**

"I didn't find any disadvantages when I went to school - didn't find it difficult to mix with people."   **Heather**

For Olivia, going to school for the first time at the age of 10, things were not so straightforward:

"I was ahead academically in the early days and that was embarrassing until I started getting on socially and doing worse in class because I wanted to fit in with my friends and they were bunking off all the time."

Mandy's brief school experiment met with mixed social results:

"I was getting on well with the kids. I had friends I've still got now that I met at school. It was the teachers I couldn't get on with. They were very belligerent that I was walking in and out of education. And if they said something I didn't agree with, I'd stand up and say 'What about -?'. 'Sit down and shut up!' It didn't grab me. Lessons I enjoyed I always turned up for but if I didn't like something I wouldn't go. It was the petty rules as well. I dyed me hair orange one day...got hauled up. To me, the colour of me hair had nothing to do with my work."

Mandy, at 14, had enough sense of self to be able to make friends without sacrificing her personality, an element which seems to have been missing in Olivia's experience at 10. Those going to FE or sixth-form college were perhaps also secure in their identity, having been able to explore it in the course of home education. This may be why most had no problems fitting in socially, with the extra benefit that their specific goals and additional maturity made it possible for them to put up with annoying parts of the regime or simply ignore them in a non-confrontational way:

"I had very poor attendance when I did my GCSEs...I used to take weeks off at a time - I'd be reading or sleeping or if it was sunny I'd feel it was better to go swimming in the sea."

The experience of being with people of different ages during his home education came in useful for Laurence on starting college:

> *"I was about four foot eleven and the men were six foot, so I was obviously different. But I survived, had lots of good friends, I'm still in contact with people from those days. There was a three year age gap - I was 14 and most of them had done their GCSEs. I got teased for being younger but I used to give as good as I got."*

Charlie, who thought he might experience racism, also settled well socially, (at the same college, coincidentally, the Taylor girls had gone to):

> *"Apart from two Asians, me and my sister were the only 'different' people. I don't think I found it a problem. It was a bit hard at first because it was new but most people were in the same boat - the friends they'd known had dropped out of school or weren't going to college. I had this group of people I could sit with and talk to. We had the same classes for three years so it was fun."*

Only one of the interviewees felt there had been a problem with college social life:

> *"I went there early - I was more mature but less socially able than the other students."* Andrew

By the time the interviewees were at university, fitting in socially was not an issue for them. They led typical student lives, with no suggestion of home education having had anything other than a positive effect on their social ability. George talked about his involvements at Bangor:

> *"I spent two years living in a chaplaincy. It's a procession of people banging on your door because they can't get the chaplain. You can't turn people away when they're in a state. Thankfully, I had friends I could go to, to sort myself out, and the network's still going, we still meet up."*

Laurence's social life at Cambridge was contrastingly hedonistic:

> *"I enjoyed the formal balls - and I ended up President of the Drinking Society - we had a couple of outings a week, a dozen*

blokes, a dozen women. You go out and have a really big night. Loads of parties, loads of fun. There's so many people I've met that plod along or don't do anything because it might be uncool."

Daniel talked about how he fitted in after university with fellow-workers from a different background:

"I worked as a builder for three years. It was a really good game. To start with they thought, 'Hey, what are you doing?' But I worked as hard as them, I was prepared to have a laugh - and we got on absolutely fine."

I may have laboured the social normality point a little - but as the issue of supposed isolation leading to an inability to fit in to society is without doubt the commonest and most erroneous of the misgivings expressed about home-based education, I feel it cannot be over-emphasised.

What was the reaction of school children and teachers to your way of life?

We have seen from Mandy's experience that teachers could be hostile to someone making flexible use of the system. Her resistance to rules cannot have helped the situation. They may have felt her attitude might be contagious, in which case all hell would break loose.

Where home educated people attended school or college for the purpose of gaining qualifications, and were prepared to tolerate small silly things for the sake of the bigger goal, teachers were often interested and helpful:

"There were a couple of teachers who singled me out as a prodigy - ridiculous. Put me in the top stream and used me as an example. One teacher was fascinated - she was wondering where I got my ideas from."   Olivia

"The lecturers were brilliant. I'm still in touch with them - the college has just written asking me to do a piece for their brochure. They were really supportive: didn't make a big thing of the fact that I was different but at the same time catered for it."   Laurence

There could be problems with higher authorities, as Emma and Flora found:

"The Principal said he was taking a risk because I hadn't got exams or any sort of record. Throughout the two and a half years I was on three months' trial. I had to be exceptionally good or I'd be kicked out. But all the teachers I had, particularly for the creative stuff, thought it was great, something different." Flora

Other interviewees suggested that being home educated was actually an advantage in applying to college or university. (This seems to be more and more the case in America.) As there is greater experience of home educated people on FE and HE courses, suspicion lessens:

"I think the fact that I hadn't been to school was a positive thing for the people who interviewed me. Everybody was a bit surprised, but you stand out. I don't think it did me any harm at all." Paul

"In three years I'd gone from thinking I might never get any GCSEs to university in Oxford. The authorities were interested in my education and in some ways I think it helped me get in. Because you have to work so much on your own here, and I'd proved that I could do that, it helped." Kate

(Maybe this point about independent working accounts for what seems a disproportionately large number of Oxbridge students amongst the interviewees: 3 out of the 15 who went to university.)

Heather was more cynical:

"Broadcasting was a new course and it seemed they'd picked one of each type of person! A black person, a Chinese person, a mature student, somebody with a baby, somebody in a suit, somebody scruffy! Somebody who'd been home educated, somebody from Luxembourg!"

Children and, later, fellow students, tended to react with disbelief and envy:

"Other students are very interested. Some of them are jealous: 'Wow! You didn't have to go to school?' I've never

had anything negative. I can't think of anyone who disagreed
with it."   Kate

It appears that going to school was not an issue that affected
children's social lives locally:

"I suppose you always get, 'Oh, you're lucky', but I don't
remember it being difficult."   Pippa

What sort of social life do you lead now?

Readers will not be surprised, by now, to know that between them
the interviewees exhibited very much the range of lifestyles and
social choices one might expect from a random group of twenty
and thirty-somethings.   Some lived alone, some with long-term
partners, three were living with their parents, a few had children,
one had a step-child, one was homosexual, one was sharing a
bachelor flat and had a child who lived with his ex-partner.   Only
one of the younger generation was married.   Edward, representing
the older generation, had married for the second time.

Heather explained the factors that had influenced some of the
decisions she had made, or was making at the age of 24, about
how she wanted to live:

"I've been with the same person in a relationship since I was
16, so I wasn't spending my time at university looking for a
boyfriend or bothering about whether I looked nice rather
than whether I'd done my essay... It's difficult when you've
got little sisters - because the youngest one's only 9, it's quite
hard to go away again, you miss them.   Also my parents
moved to this house while I was at university.   It's a beautiful
house and I love being in the country.   I get claustrophobic if
I can't see the sky.   So it's thinking of something I can do,
mainly on my own, without having to live in the city again."

Sally, a single mother in her late thirties, had another unique set
of considerations affecting her plans.   These involved the amount
her daughter's father wanted to see his child, her career in
counselling, and her spare time activities on the high wire.   The
whole family, like Heather, wanted to get into the countryside,
preferably somewhere with a home-educating community.   There

was constant concern about how any of this was to be afforded. She summarised the philosophy she had evolved:

> *"With kids you've got to take it as it comes, try and work out the best situation at the time, for everybody. It's not always perfect but you make do with what you've got and get the best thing, and that changes."*

Some lifestyles were a million miles away from Sally's:

> *"Mum calls my current lifestyle 'Over the top'! She hates things like mobile phones, laptops, wearing suits. At the moment it's too social - I'm out nine nights in a row - catching up with friends, and some of it's vaguely related to work, meeting salesmen. It's work hard, play hard. The company's very much at the forefront of my mind because there's so much paperwork. The websites and the Internet is only 10 per cent - there's sales and following people up, keeping up with what's going on in the world, and accounts and VAT."* Laurence

I could fill another book with descriptions of the further variety of interviewees' lifestyles and social activities, but I will concentrate on two aspects which are particularly interesting.

Being part of a community

It was heart-warming, particularly from the point of view of contradicting allegations of insularity, to find that many of the interviewees had made substantial contributions to their community: some abroad, as Daniel described, and some at home. All of them were concerned with making things happen, rather than being passive members of a group.

> *"At university I was involved in political societies, an anti-apartheid group, Labour, a music society, organising rock gigs. I've done a lot of voluntary jobs. I worked with a physically disabled person for four months. I'm training to be a drugs counsellor and working for a mental health helpline."* Chloe

> *"I threw myself into school life. I set up this helpline for younger students who were having problems, because I thought I could use my own experiences that way."* Kate

"I work at Glastonbury Festival every year, car checking, making sure everybody gets in and out securely. It's a real challenge, the problems that come up. I enjoy thinking on my feet. I never have seen anything of the festival, but I gather it's quite popular!"   Mandy

Sometimes work for the community was not purely altruistic:

"I worked voluntarily as an Assistant Psychologist at a hospital for people with learning disabilities because I wanted to get some experience."   Pippa

Heather was doing voluntary work mainly because she wanted to help people but also to test her aptitude for a particular vocation. (Note the self-awareness, demonstrating the clear-sighted analysis of weaknesses but also strengths, which many of the interviewees developed through having time to reflect.)

"I'm doing voluntary work with the probation service - they want me to run art workshops with young offenders, which is a bit daunting...I am good at helping people. I've had a few I've helped already. I thought I'd do voluntary work to see if I could cope with some of the things that people might tell me they'd done."

I've already written about the counselling work which George put in at university, in between running the student union and helping with accommodation problems.   His sister Grace was also involved in the life of her northern university in a big way:

"Being a music department you couldn't help being involved. Choir, orchestra, chapel. I ended up being organist in the local parish. For about two years I also did some physical manipulation for a girl with cerebral palsy."

There are enough examples here of the involvement in community activities of home educated people, to disabuse anyone of the idea that this kind of education, being largely child-centred, necessarily produces individuals with no concern for others. It is, on the contrary, possible that the greater opportunities which they have to get to know themselves while they are growing up make them emotionally and practically well equipped to reach out to others as adults. This may be harder for those who have spent their school years wrestling with exterior pressures such as those of the peer group and the National Curriculum, with no leisure to come to terms with the interior pressures of their own personality.

Family relations

Apart from the two families where relationships were bad before home education started, (Kate's, where her parents had divorced, and Emma's, where there was a big disparity in intelligence between parents and daughter), all the interviewees enjoyed close friendships with their families - or with their parents at any rate, since there were two cases where they had difficulty finding common ground with their (conventionally educated) siblings:

> *"My brother and I are very different. We don't really get on, we don't have anything in common. It's hard for my brother and sister to accept my disability. They view it as a bit of a 'tragedy'."* Jim

(Jim's disability is an immobile spine, which also affects movement in one arm.)

> *"My brother's a lawyer. The world he lives in is populated by very wealthy people - if you're not a winner, you're a loser. Obviously, because I'm one of the family, I'm not a loser, I'm just a weirdo eccentric going off and doing my own thing."* Daniel

Some had gone through a bad patch. Many children who have pioneered the trail out of the nest will recognise this scenario:

> *"I've always had a very good relationship with my parents. The only stormy patch was my first year at university, going from being at home all the time to being at Cambridge, being independent, and being in Nottingham during the holidays working, and being in London. Never being at home. The old, 'you treat this place like a hotel'. I'm very close to my parents now. I speak to them a couple of times a week. It's not like your parents, it's very informal."* Laurence

There were many other comments along the lines of the following from Harriet: *"I get on really well with my parents now. Couldn't be closer, really."*

It is impossible to say whether this is an effect of the understanding developed over the home education years, or whether such a mutually considerate and affectionate relationship made home education feasible and desirable in the first place.

There are three important strands to the evidence about the social and emotional aspects of home education presented in this chapter. First, it appears that many of those interviewed were more mature, emotionally and socially, than their schooled contemporaries. Harriet, for instance, was allowed into theatre school two years early because it was felt she had the maturity to cope, and the same was true of Laurence's and Andrew's admission to FE college. Several of the interviewees reported that their teenage friends were a few years older than themselves. Part of this may be due to the time for reflection referred to above and part to the greater opportunities for experience of the adult world which most of those interviewed enjoyed:

> *"When I went to university I'd already been living on my own, on and off, since I was 15, 16, so I'd done all the drinking and staying up late, whereas a lot of people had just left home and were excessive about everything."*   Heather

Secondly, it was clear that family interest and support were essential to a healthy social and emotional life. One of the interviewees who educated herself without help from her parents, after refusing to go to school, felt that home education was restrictive socially, and she had missed out by rejecting the companionship of school.

Lastly, it may not be too fanciful to suggest that the models of teacher and learner in home educating families could break the vicious circle of conformity-rewarding teacher/pupil roles which reinforce a national ethos of intolerance towards children in each generation. A different kind of adult/child relationship, in which mutual respect in learning fosters self-esteem and empathy, might affect home educated children's grown-up behaviour as parents and/or teachers. (Chapter 6 examines the evidence.)

Chapter five

Work worth doing

*"A life worth living and work worth doing - that is what I want
for children (and all people), not just, or not even, something
called 'a better education'."*
John Holt *"A life worth living"*

John Holt, the American thinker and writer on home education,
believed strongly in the value of satisfying work for children as
well as adults. (See his *Escape from Childhood*, ch.18, for a fuller
explanation of this philosophy than is possible here.)

While recognising the damage done by exploitative child labour
in some countries, he proposed that work could be a useful part of
a child's life from several points of view: as a way to learn skills
in a real-life situation, with its unpredictable problems and
mixture of fellow workers of all ages; as a way to explore part of
the adult world and become proficient in using its tools, which are
often not available to children; as a way to develop self-esteem in
the course of carrying out a job which others recognise as useful;
and, of course, to earn some money, which tends to bring with it a
sense of power and self-respect in our consumer society.

Holt's thoughts on worthwhile work, as opposed to work that
relates purely to its buying capacity, foreshadowed the current
attempts at 'downshifting' being made by those who feel that the
pursuit of a financially well-rewarded, but stressful, career is
dominating their lives. Although part of the plan is usually to
make more time for areas of life outside work, it often includes an
effort to find forms of work that are more fulfilling spiritually,
intellectually or physically, and that promote good family and
community relationships through an easier integration into
everyday life.

A recent article in the journal Holt founded, *Growing without Schooling*, emphasised how such an approach to work could be helpful to home-educating families, both as a way of showing children that jobs do not have to be for life, or highly paid, to be worth doing, and as a way of organising parents' work to leave time for being with the children. ('Adults: Liberate Yourselves ...' Michael Fogler, on 'un-jobbing', *GWS* 124, Sept/Oct 98). It can, of course, work the other way: as I have mentioned elsewhere, several parents found their own 'work worth doing' through having been involved in home education.

Many of the people I interviewed had invented or discovered work which interested them, not necessarily permanently, before the age at which children normally turn their minds to such things. (For convenience, I will define this rather arbitrarily as 16.) Having the time and the freedom to pursue it, they were able to make the most of whatever learning experiences this work entailed, and to lay the foundations of self-discipline and awareness necessary to a fulfilling adult working life. As well as discussing these jobs and how they found them, I shall look at whether, as adults, they feel themselves to have 'work worth doing' and, if so, how they approached the business of establishing it.

Have they felt a need to stick at one thing, or have they tried lots of options? Do they follow several paths at once, each on a part-time basis? Were qualifications or experience or personal contact the crucial factor, if there was one, in getting work? And finally, what can we make, in the light of what they say, of the suggestion that home educated children will not be able to get up in the mornings and succeed in the world of work because they have not had the preparation for it which school is supposed to be?

What kinds of work were you involved in as a child, and what benefits do you think there were to this experience?

Because 'school-leaving age' has no meaning in the context of home-based education, one of the interviewees opted for full-time work before the age at which it's normally undertaken. The family were presumably prepared to dress this up as a form of educative work experience, had the authorities questioned its legality - not hard to do since she was learning numerous practical skills:

"I went to work at 14 because I was sick of education. Big row with my mother because she wanted me to take some exams and I wasn't interested. I went and worked with a local painter and decorator for three years. I earned money then, bought myself a motor-bike and nice clothes. At 14 I didn't know what I wanted to do. I thought 'Oh, I'll have a look about the world, see what I want to do'. I wasn't one of these people who know at 16 they want to be a doctor. I've got my whole life ahead of me, so if I want to be a doctor I'll go to sixth form college and get my O and A levels and go to university."   Mandy

She knew what she was letting herself in for, having already worked part-time in various capacities:

"We're in a lambing area and I'd go up every spring and help out round the farms. I started that when I was about 12, 13. I got friendly with a farmer's wife and she said, 'I could really do with some help around the house and with the pet lambs'. So I used to go up and live with them for a month, over April, and I'd do the housework and the washing-up and cook the tea and feed the pet lambs and the dog and cat, and all the stuff she didn't have time for at that time of year. I loved it, it was great. And I used to help on a stall in the market on Fridays. I was a waitress and general dogsbody at a guesthouse. I lived down there for two or three months."

There are several interesting points to make about Mandy's varied experience of work as a child. First, she was out and about a lot in the course of her daily life and therefore open to the opportunities that came along. She had the social skill to make local contacts leading to work, and the self-confidence which suggested to prospective employers that she might be the right person for the job, even at 12 or 13. She was secure enough to live happily away from home for quite long periods at this age, and able to take on responsible jobs which would normally be the province of an adult. She also had the self-discipline to get to work on time and put in the required hours, despite finding this difficult during her short school attendance, (suggesting that, as with learning, motivation is everything). Laurence also did serious work from an early age, but on a self-employed basis, showing a talent for entrepreneurial projects which later formed part of his business activities as a young man:

"I've run businesses since I was nine. I had a sweet shop then. When I was eleven Dad came home one day and all the lettuces had gone. I'd sold them to the greengrocer's down the road. When I was about twelve I had one where there was a disused quarry and they had a load of round clay pipes. I phoned the company that had bought them and said, 'I want to buy your clay pipes for five pence each'. This guy took me seriously and let me buy them so I sent a cheque for £20 and put a concrete base in the bottom and sold them as flower pots. Made a couple of hundred pounds."

The importance of serendipity, and the lateral thinking that goes with it, crops up again here, together with being out and about in the real world enough to spot where the opportunities lie. As was the case with Mandy at a similar age, Laurence obviously had the social skills to persuade his buyers, and the seller of the pipes, that he had a good proposition. He also had sufficient confidence to make the approach in the first place. Both qualities were probably reinforced by success, encouraging further ventures.

Harriet emphasised that the process of working itself could generate self-esteem, (as Holt suggested):

"I started doing a lot of puppet work at children's birthday parties and things - I was only 12 and 13 then. I was helping to make the puppets and operate them, and do the voices. I got interviewed in newspapers - it was good and it did give me confidence."

Edward found the continual movement involved in his working life as a teenager often gave him the opportunity to try out other forms of work when he was not performing, extending both his self-directed learning and his appreciation of what possible careers might entail:

"When we were in pantomime my companions were the chorus girls. One evening something had cropped up and we were

laughing, and I'd said something about some chemistry or other: a man comes over and says, 'Oh, are you interested in chemistry?', so I said 'Well, ye-es', and it turned out he was the hydrologist for the North of England area. He said, 'Like to come and work in my laboratory for the next couple of weeks?' I was thrilled to bits. And often you'd meet people, they'd take an interest. A photographer up in Newcastle-upon-Tyne came round taking pictures of us on the stage, brought the photographs round, got into conversation about these interests I had, in zoology, and photography. The next moment we were corresponding while I was travelling round, and whenever we went to Newcastle along I'd go and see him, and he'd take me out on some of his assignments. I remember once going round photographing pets in the back alleys."

These sorts of opportunities to experience different types of work, without the adult financial responsibilities which might inhibit risk-taking, are valuable ones, quite apart from what we might call their character-building aspect, and their potential for increasing technical, psychological and intellectual understanding of the world from which schooled children are excluded for so much of the time, until they are suddenly expected to find a place in it. Furthermore, they can form the nucleus of a network of personal contacts which might someday be useful.

How have you found satisfying work as an adult? (and did you try out many possibilities on the way?)

Following on from the previous section's suggestion that many people like to 'look about the world', in Mandy's words, before deciding on adult work, it was interesting to see that hardly any of the interviewees had settled early on one job which they felt would be for life. This is very much in accord with modern economic thinking, which predicts that most people will have more than one career, that part-time working will increase, and that people will find themselves training and re-training as the demand for skills changes throughout their working life. (See for example, Charles Handy's *The Empty Raincoat*.)

All those with a strong early feeling for their own 'work worth doing' were in the creative field, and traced their ambitions back to elements of their home education:

> *"When I was little I wanted to be all sorts of things to do with art, but then I started getting into film. I've made films and videos. I've got friends who do it informally, little independent things, and through college I've got access to all this equipment so I've been doing a lot of film and TV work."*
>
> Olivia

It was perhaps fortunate that she had this inner conviction about what she ought to be doing, since the careers guidance at her secondary school seems to have been less than helpful:

> *"They told me to be a night-watchman or something in an art gallery or something ridiculous like that: go-go dancer! They had a computer programme."*

I have discussed, in previous chapters, how Chloe and Andrew developed their interests in poetry-writing and film respectively, and how Edward's work as a teenager, drawing and photographing in museums and the natural world, eventually led to a fulfilling job in biological illustration. As in the pursuit of home-based learning, serendipity played its part in the direction of each person's work:

> *"I settled down to work at the University Museum. Work started to roll in. I just fitted in to everything - I was at home. Then the thing outgrew itself: I had so much stuff coming in from various publishers, I went free-lance for about thirteen years, but eventually I had seen that economically it was going downhill so I came to the university biology department here as an illustrator. It wasn't going to lead to anything really wonderful but it was stable. Then along comes Maurice Baxter and he said, 'How would you like to do a doctorate?' I said, 'I'll have to think very carefully about that. I haven't got the basic academic requirements'. 'Well' he said, 'they're not **absolutely** necessary'. It took me about five and a half years part-time. I wanted to finish it before I retired from here. It was about polymorphism in bi-valve molluscs, the mechanism that sustains variation, in relation to predation and environmental factors. It was an area of major*

interest to Maurice and I'd been doing a lot of work with him on this subject. Not just illustration - he used to come and have long chats. It was the biggest surprise to me: I didn't ever think this sort of thing would happen, but I accepted because of my interest in it and because, going back to childhood, I always wanted to <u>do</u> something."

Most interviewees tried their hand at many things before becoming as devoted to one area as those above. Chloe's talent for writing led her down a cul-de-sac before she discovered what she really wanted to do, but she did not see this as a completely negative experience:

"I wanted to become a journalist so I applied for a place and in the meantime came down here to Bristol, did four months' voluntary work in a homeless hostel and found that was really what I wanted to do. I went to the course anyway, and realised it wasn't for me - an expensive way of realising that, and now I've got a big loan to pay off. It was the only way I could find out, I suppose. I'm now really into the caring professions - I feel like I'm finally into what I want to do and it's going quite well."

I mentioned in the previous chapter that voluntary activities were the medium through which many of the interviewees found the work they considered worth doing. For some, they were also a necessary first step in their chosen career, a way of gaining experience and getting known: a common pattern nowadays. After leaving university Daniel had jobs in several different areas, which he felt he learnt a lot from, before returning to higher education so that he could develop the interest in environmental management he has become increasingly committed to, to the extent of currently working in it for nothing:

"I started my own business. I had loads of mates who were doing various different things like carpet-fitting and bricklaying. I ended up giving them a hand and picked up lots of skills on the way. It was really therapeutic, doing practical stuff after years of mental stuff. (A point also made by Heather, later in the chapter.) *I'd never have done building if my father hadn't been quite practically inspired and I'd had the time to learn enough skills off him not to be afraid to go*

out there and have a go at doing it myself. And because I liked buildings I went and became an estate agent. Learnt a lot about people: some not very nice things about people, and I picked up the business about selling yourself to other people and that it's professionally part of your job to make the other person feel at ease, that sort of empathy. Anyway, I hated it towards the end and decided to do this M.Sc. in Land Resource Management at Silsoe and was fortunate, because of the other things I'd done, to have a few grand to allow me to do so. Now I'm working down here as a volunteer botanical surveyor for the Somerset Environmental Records Centre, with training half a day or one day a week - talks from people like the Mammal Society or spider specialists. There are some complete screaming nutters out there - people who get terribly excited about lichen. Now as far as I'm concerned, lichen schmichen! But I'm quite happy to go. I hope I will be able to do something in it - I've got no problem with doing just about any job. I'll always have an environmental interest - I think I'll end up being one of those completely barking mad loonies, but I haven't quite decided in what yet!"

A combination of technical competence, wide work experience before and during university, natural business nous, and the gift of the gab, enabled Laurence to set up a profitable company within months of graduating. His degree was only tangentially relevant, (it included a course on small businesses), and his area of expertise, website design, more or less chose him through a chance comment at a job interview and forty-eight hours of the ultimate self-directed learning:

"I didn't know what a web page looked like but I thought it can't be that difficult. So two days and two nights, lots of magazines, lots of books, lots of cups of coffee, I wrote this website!"

His view of the relative value of practical and academic education is interesting:

"I spent a year with an audio company, in the testing lab. An amazing boss who let me make mistakes. Not the big mistakes, but he would let me make the little mistakes so you could learn. I was responsible for making all the test hardware for

the company and I learnt so much in that year, more in that year than in four years at Cambridge in terms of the real stuff."

Heather made a similar point:

"After A levels I decided I wanted to learn a few practical things, give my brain a rest from academic things, so I worked as a kind of secretary for a year, with Dad, running his office - it's a mail-order business - desk-top publishing, learning how to use computers, type. Because I thought 'Otherwise, I'm going to finish university and I'm not going to know how to type or fax or ...'"

George and Grace both abandoned their original career interests, Grace because on investigation she felt the training for psychology would be too long and too rigid intellectually, and George because the funding for jobs in forestry dried up. Both had other strong interests and the flexibility of mind that enabled them to switch paths:

"At the time I was also looking into church liturgy, and I was advised to study music for that, something I'd been vigorously struggling against for ages because it was almost a hobby, it wasn't something I thought of in those terms - so I decided to study it with something else but at the end of the first year I dropped the theology and the religious studies. While I was there I was considered fairly good at composition, which was why I ended up doing the M.A. "   Grace

George had done a fair amount of voluntary work in the Forest of Dean and Grizedale as well as his forestry degree but, because of the prospective employment situation, decided, like his sister, to get another qualification and change tack:

"Quite a few forestry jobs had disappeared off the face of the earth, so I trogged off to York to do a Master's in biological computation. I did my project doing research for the Forestry Commission but just at the end of that year they announced swingeing cuts in the grant aid for biological research - so back to the job pool again, with about a five grand debt! I got a job almost immediately, with the Health and Safety Executive. "

He wastes no time on regrets about having to give up his childhood ambition and clearly feels he has found his own 'work worth doing', even if, like Laurence, he found it more by luck than judgement:

"If I had gone straight into forestry I'd probably be happy doing what I was doing. But what I'm doing now: it's advice, a bit of enforcement work, and you see immediate results. You go into a site that's an absolute tip and have a couple of arguments or a nice quiet chat and when you go back a couple of weeks later the place is an infinitely better place to work and you can start on the health issues. You feel as though you're doing something."

In the very structured environment of a government organisation, George's qualifications and performance at a standard interview were crucial to his being offered the job:

"It's a tatty bits of paper society, so if that's the way the rules are I will play the rules. That doesn't mean I agree with them."

Many interviewees pointed out that by this stage in life your type of primary and secondary education has become irrelevant, so you are not likely to reap any direct kudos from having been educated at home, as people applying to further and higher education establishments appear to have done. But the indirect benefits, in terms of making use of good, often exceptional, social skills; knowledge of the adult world; willingness to learn, and the ability to do so flexibly and appropriately, all seemed to be a help to those looking for work in less formal environments.

A word about what people valued in their work, what made it worth doing for them. The majority appeared not to be in it primarily for the money - even Laurence, who manifested some of the outward trappings of a Yuppie, seemed more excited by the challenge of working hard and solving problems than by the possibility of making a profit.

So what else did people look for in their work? Many, as discussed earlier, wanted to help others in some way. Some, like Grace, had an outstanding creative talent or interest that they wanted to pursue through work eventually, and were happy to do less interesting jobs, part-time, to finance it. This applied also to those with a passion for travel, like Mollie and Paul, and those trying to finance their studies, like Charlie:

> *"I've been an ice-cream salesman, driving a mobile ice-cream van. That was hard work but it was good fun. It was a summer holiday job, to pay off the overdraft."*

Some needed the satisfaction of doing something technical or practical. Some wanted, essentially, variety, and perhaps some sort of spiritual fulfilment in their work. Mandy suggested this in a quote that conveys well the endless possibilities open to the home educated and the welcome element of romance which can attend this freedom, something completely absent from many work situations and scoffed at by those who consider that work, like school, is inevitably soul-destroying and rarely 'worth doing' in Holt's sense:

> *"Through Education Otherwise I had a job crab and lobster fishing in the far north of Scotland. Someone needed a hand and I was free and he said, 'Oh, just what I want. Come on up!' Me big chance to do that! - and that was wonderful, one of the best jobs I've ever had. The scenery was stunning - getting out onto the loch, just as the sun comes up, about six o'clock in the morning - this beautiful sunrise, the deer on the headland, otters and seals in the sea. It was hard work but it was really beautiful."*

Do you have plans for future work? How have these developed from what you're doing now?

Some of those interviewed were at a point where they were thinking about new options, having recently finished higher education or become interested in a different area from their current work. Heather's thoughts about this indicate the extent to which society expects people to conform to certain working patterns:

> *"The problem is you get a lot of pressure about having a 'career'. Not from my parents, more from my friends. Especially if you're female - to do with toeing the line for the feminist side by doing something stressful and well-paid! Or*

worthy. I have ideas but I'm not very good at making my mind up about things. I thought about what I'd actually done for my degree and trying to get a job working in television but I found it was rather superficial - not everybody, obviously, but I think you have to be very motivated, committed to that one thing, which I'm not. I'm more a dabbler in different things."

As well as the voluntary activities with the probation service mentioned in a previous chapter she did, in fact, work, but not in a conventional 9-5 way:

"I help with the education of the little ones, and I work for a lady who has a mail-order fruitcake business, so I make cakes most mornings a couple of hours a day. I work in the post office on Sundays. Things are quite difficult here at the moment for my parents, so I'm sticking around a bit to try and help. Dad lost his job and he's got his Industrial Tribunal this week."

This collection of paid, unpaid and family activities is exactly the kind of 'work worth doing' Holt wrote about: what a shame its worth is so little recognised that Heather felt it was somehow unsatisfactory in the long-term.

Sally had a similar lifestyle but seemed more at ease with it, though she also worried about how to manage it in the future:

"There's been three strands really, the sort of performance and circuses strand, and the counselling strand, and the children strand. I suppose I'm aiming towards bringing them together. I've got dreams of a sort of centre where people can come and do theatre but in a therapeutic way. I've got to finish the counselling course first and then maybe I could get a job two or three days a week and we could live in the country but near enough to a town."

Another interviewee, Emma, was also at a transitional stage. She had grown tired of teaching piano, a job she had fallen into through taking on the younger pupils of her own teacher, and she had also become increasingly interested in working with people with learning disabilities, having become an Advocate for one such person. She and a friend had decided to cut back their other work and set up a residential care home, taking family needs into consideration, as those discussed above had done. Perhaps home education disposes people to give these a high priority when thinking about how to integrate 'work worth doing' with the rest of their lives?

"We're only registered for two people. We had a resident last year but he moved on because he needed more intensive help than we offer, so we're waiting for our next resident. It's been a bit chaotic: the day after we registered, my mother died. My grandmother, who she was looking after, is still alive, so Gran's had to come and live with me, and then we had to move house because we didn't have a big enough house to run the care home and Gran. The residents come from the Adult Placement Scheme - the social services refer to them, and they have a number of homes in the county that do this kind of thing, and they match people up. I think I'll always teach piano a bit, keep it going, but I'm winding it down slowly."

Jim's thoughts about the future were complicated by his disability. He had developed an interest in medical engineering since leaving Cambridge and was hoping to do a Ph.D. in it, or get a job, after he finished his part-time M.Sc. His plans were probably more uncertain than most, because he did not know the cause of, or the prognosis for, his physical problems, but, generally, few of the interviewees had the rigid expectations of future work which would have been common a couple of generations ago. Charlie, an undergraduate studying hotel management, had a typical view:

"I'm terribly short-term in my goals. I've a friend who looks five years ahead: 'I'm going to have this job; I'm going to get married', whereas me, I just look to the end of the year, finishing my placement at the hotel here, then my course. I don't seem to think far ahead. It clouds it too much."

With one or two exceptions, the interviewees embraced the modern uncertainty and all its possibilities with enthusiasm, feeling themselves well equipped to take advantage of whatever changing opportunities for 'work worth doing' might come their way.

It appears from this evidence of what home educated people are doing now or plan to do in the future, that there is an enormous variety to their choice of fulfilling work, with perhaps a slight bias in favour of caring or creative activities. None had become a conventional school teacher, though many taught as part of their job, and were presumably rather successful at it, having thought long and hard about the way people learn best.

It is reassuring, from the point of view of those who suggest that home educators may attempt to indoctrinate their children with a certain lifestyle, to reflect that none of the interviewees had gone into the same line of work as their parents, unless you count Mandy's job in the family candle-making business. And, from the point of view of those who see school as an absolutely necessary preparation for the rough, tough world of work, let it be noted that not one of the interviewees could in any sense be described as unemployed.

Chapter six

Thinking outside the box

"The university was looking for someone to revamp their approach to education. They knew I had homeschooled my children and that I continue to work in the homeschooling movement. I had definite ideas about empowering students to capitalise on their own strengths. I spoke about the value of projects, of letting children mature on their own timetables, of trusting children and teachers... The system is tough to alter, but I know that I am planting living seeds in my students of what possibilities there are in education when we think outside of our box. I'm gratified that my own three are great at thinking outside the box, even when living inside boxes by choice, (going to schools and colleges)."

Jacque Ensign,

Growing Without Schooling 118, Sept/Oct 97, p18-19

This chapter is about the effect that being home educated has had on my interviewees' thinking about education. Have they, like the children of the American education professor quoted above, learnt to 'think outside the box'? If so, it is possible that their views may influence local educational provision in little ways and that such an effect would be magnified if applied to the much larger numbers of people being home educated now.

I have described how individuals have been able to persuade institutions to alter their practice on an ad hoc basis - for example, to allow someone to attend sixth-form college two years early or to do more exam subjects in a year than usually allowed. Perhaps one of the influences home educated people might exert would be towards further flexibility, so that pre-16 education began to resemble adult provision. The 14-plus initiative providing FE courses for teenagers who find the school curriculum does not suit

; to be a step in the right direction, but generally there is a huge contrast in policy towards the two sectors. Before 16, everything is prescribed or proscribed: certain subjects students must follow; certain grades they must get to pursue certain sixth-form courses; vast areas of potential interest not open to them at all; and, of course, the widespread though erroneous perception that all this is compulsory.

In adult education there is a different ethos - mainly because of the competitive aspect to funding dependent on voluntary attendance, rather than a belief in an alternative educational philosophy. Nevertheless, the effect is one of openness, encouragement, a willingness to take into account evidence of experience or abilities where formal qualifications are lacking, a student-centred approach to the selection of subjects, and a range of ways in which courses can be studied: through distance learning, part-time or full-time attendance or a combination of some sort. There are university access courses, facilities for part-time research, one-day workshops, module-based courses that allow people to go off and do something else for a year and then pick up the threads again.

Parents whose own education has taught them to question why their children's schools cannot be more like this, may start to change them through their involvement. If they are home educating themselves, they may influence others to do the same, or at least to think in new ways about the purpose and methods of school. So what reflections did the interviewees have on their experience and its relationship to conventional education? What did they consider the benefits and drawbacks of home-based learning, and are they planning it for their own young families?

What were the benefits of being home educated, as they seem to you now?

Several of those who had been entirely home educated made the same point - that it is difficult to establish what would have been different had they been to school:

> *"To ask Grace and me, in particular, the disadvantages is a little odd because we haven't had enough experience of the*

mainstream system to have really direct comparison." George

"I can't say - if I had been put through the formal system I might have been a complete Wally." Edward

Laurence clearly believes that the serendipitous element of his education has been significant but cannot imagine the outcome of an alternative way of life:

"I don't wish that I hadn't been home educated because so many consequences and coincidences - this led to this led to this - have led to work for me. I do believe I would be different if I'd been to school. How, and whether it would be better or worse, is a different thing! Almost by definition I'd be happy with the me that I'd become either way. "

It is also difficult to establish whether positive effects on career or sociability or anything else are due directly to home education, since so many other factors must be taken into consideration:

"A lot of the advantages I gained from home education were things I have seen other people not gain from going to school. It's difficult to decide what is to do with their education and what is to do with the person or their background." Daniel

"I don't know whether being taught at home has had much effect on the way I've gone. I think I would have been quite shy if I'd gone to school - and I'm not shy. But there's so many other things that happen that have a big effect on your life." Heather

Those who have greater experience of orthodox education are perhaps more aware of the specific benefits of home-based learning, both short- and long-term. These fall into three groups: personality development, learning advantages, and support in potentially difficult social situations. For two interviewees, it was important to have time to develop self-awareness and emotional strength:

"We had to put my emotional well-being before anything else. I was terrified of going and it just got worse. They sent me off to child guidance and it was hopeless. They weren't sympathetic at all. They were trying to find problems in the

t weren't there and just creating more problems."
Kate

Many interviewees reported that they felt an independence and a self-confidence that they suspected was untypical of their schooled contemporaries:

"If I see something that I want to do I'll go and do it. I'll try it: the confidence to go and try something myself, even though I wouldn't say that I'm an overly confident person -it's self-worth."
Mandy

One aspect of this self-confidence was a lack of fear of authority:

"I didn't have authority thrown at me at school so I tend to behave quite informally with people. O.K. they're my boss, they can tell me what's what. That's what they're paid to do, and I'm paid to listen. That's not going to mean I'm going to spend the whole time in awe of somebody unless I'm led to believe they're particularly deserving of awe."
Daniel

Related to this is a form of personal integrity - the independence of mind to resist following the crowd, a first step towards the creative processes involved in 'thinking outside the box':

"It was a good time to be out of school, because it's the worst time to be __in__ school, when everyone's at that awful age and there's a lot of peer pressure. I never had that and I think that was good for me. I have a quite different attitude to a lot of my friends. They've been in the system for so long that they're very tied to it - for me to take this year out, it's just taking a year out, I'll get my degree next year, but for other people it's, 'I'm 21, I've got to get my degree this year because this is the way it happens'."
Kate

"It sounds cheesy but it's a belief in doing the right thing rather than the official thing. Not doing something because somebody says you do it but doing it because it makes sense. And if you're worried that people are laughing, just doing it. I'm less worried by peer pressure I suppose. I don't mind doing things that one 'shouldn't' do."
Laurence

Self-esteem derives partly from confidence in the ability to learn and feeling able to tackle new things, as Mandy's comment implied and as Holt tried to explain to educators. The development of self-reliance and self-discipline in learning had been important to the interviewees:

> "It allowed me to work more independently, which I think is one of the best things it's done for me - it's essential, really, to work for yourself. I could carry on easily at university, which is where it hits most people because A levels are more structured." Pippa

> "I think the main benefit was will-power - **having** to be dedicated. It gave me a love of learning so when I'm studying I enjoy it. When I was at home I knew I didn't <u>have</u> to because there was no-one checking me, so I did it out of choice and kept that love of learning." Kate

This recalls Daniel's comment on how compulsion affects motivation. He went on to say:

> "I perhaps am slightly more disciplined than the average as regards learning things myself. If I need to find out about something, I go and get books out and I'm self-primed. When I went to FE college, but mainly when I went to university, I couldn't believe how easy it was. Somebody came in and they told you all the answers! "

> "It's being creative, thinking about things for yourself. When I got to doing my A levels I found my background was a big benefit because I could think on my own. Other people, once they got to the independent stage of their education, after GCSEs, had a few more problems with doing things for themselves, thinking for themselves." Mollie

> "There's the flexible approach - that you **can** adapt. And you're used to being in charge of your own learning, so it's not a novelty - you're not shoved in at the deep end, and sink or swim." Grace

Some interviewees mentioned specific ways in which learning benefited from being in a home education environment:

> "I think it's important to spend a lot of time playing when you're little because you have so much stress later on. It doesn't hold you back in any way later." Mollie

*ie biggest advantages was having a great range of
..... that you can do - learning through other
environments, not just sitting at a desk."* Pippa

*"It was the ability to explore something and not do it if I
didn't like it but really throw myself into it if I did."* Chloe

The area of support for difficult social situations relates mainly to
the experience of bullying in school, but one could also draw the
wider conclusion that the strong family unit typical of most of
these home educators' childhoods provided security during their
forays into the outside world. Charlie's comment, *"It's made me
grow really close to my family,"* was one of many on the same
theme.

As far as bullying was concerned, the obvious benefit of home
education was that it removed children from the source of the
trouble and offered them somewhere to learn without having their
concentration disturbed by fear. Two people felt that being home
educated had forestalled any problems there might have been with
bullying:

*"I'd either have been a bully or been bullied. I'd have had to
stick up for meself."* Mandy

"I'm black. Maybe I missed having the racial harassment."
Charlie

Taking a child out of school because of bullying, whether to be
home educated or to go to a different school, is seen by some as
undesirable: children should learn to fight back in preparation for
the real world. There is no evidence from the interviewees who
left because of bullying that they are less able to cope with the
social and psychological difficulties of life, than those who did not
attend for other reasons. Needless to say though, interviewees did
report **some** disadvantages to home education. These were mostly
on the themes of initial social isolation, which some people had to
work hard to overcome, and a hotchpotch of missing academic
skills.

Olivia felt that primary school would have given her different
ways of behaving:

"I got an extra-good start academically. Maybe not socially. It's not like I was sheltered - I met other little children, but I didn't get as good a start. When you go to school your role models are your peer group and you want to be like them and they influence you a lot. My parents influenced me more than anyone else. I was trying to be like them and looking to them for example. If I'd been to school I'd be a very different person."

It is interesting that Olivia sees this lack of conformity with her peers as a bad thing, whereas some of the interviewees quoted above saw it as a benefit of home education. Perhaps it was peculiarly difficult for her to fit in suddenly to the school culture at the age of 10 or 11, with puberty on the horizon and all her age-mates trying to adjust to the demands of secondary school.

Those who had left school because of the uncomfortable social environment complained more about isolation at home than those who were home educated early on. This seems paradoxical, but could either be because they were used to the physical presence of lots of people, or because their parents were not as tuned in to the possibilities for providing a social life outside school as those who educated at home from principle. I have already discussed Kate's view of her social life during home education, the most negative put forward. Jim also felt that the possibilities for socialising as a home educator were fewer in those days:

"For me, it was a minor disadvantage that I've got over. The disadvantage was far outweighed by the advantage of not being at school, but the result was that when I was 16 I was naive about other people. I get the impression that it's better now, because there are so many people doing it that there are networks, and I think that's brilliant. That obviously solves the problem."

As far as missing academic skills are concerned, the experience of individuals was patchy, with no uniformity to the problems.

"At the time I wasn't any good at it at school, so I don't know whether things like maths, if I'd stayed, I'd have got more of an understanding?"   Flora

"Because I was the first one they probably didn't push me as much as they might have done the others in terms of sciences, which I've occasionally regretted since. My next sister down, she's off in Africa, she's 22, she was always much more into sciences. We were naturally drawn in the direction we would have been and for me that was more creative and writing."

Chloe

Two sisters, Heather and Mollie, said their spelling was not good, though that of their equally home educated little sisters was. Mollie also said she had had trouble with exams to start with:

*"It **seems** there's a disadvantage when it gets to exams, not in reality but because you're not used to the system. By A levels I'd got the hang of it a bit better but for GCSEs I wasn't used to that way of learning things, doing things, at all. Maybe at that stage I didn't get the grades I was capable of. I did them in a year as well: I did art, English, politics, French, maths and biology."*

Kate was unaccustomed to public speaking:

"It was hard to be in classes - to speak in front of people, because for six years I'd just read on my own and thought on my own, hadn't had to present my arguments to anyone, and suddenly I was in classes of 20 - I was very self-conscious but eventually I got a lot better."

Two people regretted the lack of a particular area of the conventional curriculum:

*"Because of the hypothermia I hadn't been able to do any sport. I **love** sport now. That's the only thing I'm sad I didn't have a go at at school, but I'd probably have had some Nazi sports master who'd have made my life hell and I'd have ended up detesting it."*   Daniel

"Technology was expensive. It was harder to acquire the cutting edge of technology. But there are other ways of achieving the same thing. For example, access to experts: all you need do these days is turn on the television, or you can go to exhibitions, you can go to talks that they have in the evenings."   George

It is tempting to explain these objections on the basis of individuals' particular weaknesses or unique family circumstances, and indeed, since it seems impossible to draw any generalised conclusions about home education from them, that's exactly what I'm going to do. They were, in any case, very few compared with the perceived benefits, such as self-esteem, and discipline in learning, which were noted by several different interviewees.

Are you home educating your own children, or would you consider it?

Sally, a single parent, was adopting a flexible approach to her daughter's schooling, which she anticipated using also with her son when he became five:

> "I was thinking I'd like to move somewhere where there was some people out of school, and we could join in a little bit. She'd need to be with people her own age. I don't want her to be in school now until she's 16. It just feels like she's going into this machine really, and out the other end. But she's old enough now to make that choice and stand by it."

Her nine year old daughter compared the two sorts of learning:

> "I've gone back to school for a year now. I've got a less strict teacher who likes to have jokes and things, and I learnt joined-up writing. There was a lot more time to do things when you're out of school. I think when you're out of school you get quite as much education as when you're in school, except in different ways. Going on educational outings and workshops, and I can read every night."

Sally's brother was the only person interviewed who unequivocally ruled out home education for his two children:

> "I would not consider home education. For all their faults, schools of whatever kind give a wide spectrum of subjects, social contacts and leisure activities which if all properly funnelled give you a wider palette to later narrow your own personal interests and career and further education possibilities."

The attitude of these second generation parents and prospective parents, compared with those of very idealistic first generation home educators, is more analytical and based in reality:

"There's quite a few of my friends who have said, 'Oh, I'm definitely not sending my kids to school'. Sometimes I'm quite wary of it because there's one girl I know - she's quite a travellerish sort of person - she's only going to be teaching it what she thinks is important - very 'green' attitude but not anything else. I don't think it's going to be balanced."

Flora

Another part of this realistic attitude to home education was an appreciation of the extent to which it affected parents' own lives:

"In an ideal world I think it'd definitely be a good thing to avoid school altogether. If I was in a father role to a child I'd seriously consider not sending her to school and staying home to look after her. But I don't think, even though the education system is so bad, that people should be put in a situation where they have to give up their own possibilities of a job to do that."

Jim

The women, in particular, having developed strong personal interests and/or career ambitions through their home education, were concerned about how to balance these with the needs of their children:

"I would probably be more selfish than my parents - it's a sacrifice to say you're going to have small people around you all the time and lose out on adult company and conversation."

Heather

"I don't have time for hobbies at the moment but I'd like to write and I would like to start a theatre company off. I'm not going to seriously think about that until the youngest's at school. When they're at school I'll have my time back, and I'm quite looking forward to it really."

Harriet

"The more I talk about educating her, I start off saying 'no', and then I think, well, it's more possible these days, it would be a fun thing. I do want my own career. My Mum didn't, and she's only just getting her life back now - but your own kids are definitely worth it."

Flora

Several interviewees were in favour of sending the child to school but keeping home education as an option if it didn't work out:

"I would consider it. It was a good experience for me. There are good places so it would depend on where I was. If I found the school was really bad, I'd take them out without blinking an eye. But if I knew they were enjoying school and they weren't having any problems, yes, I'd have them in." Charlie

"I think it's a useful thing; the option should be there. If my daughter had problems at school, a learning difficulty or anything, I wouldn't let her suffer. I'd definitely take her out. The good thing about it now is there'd be a lot more understanding from other people."   Flora

Many thought home education would be the first option for them, rather than a fall-back position. All but one of those who had been completely home educated envisaged doing the same with their own children:

"I would be happy to teach them myself and I think the child would get more out of it than many get out of school. You'd have to screw up pretty badly to not be able to do a reasonably good job on a one-to-one basis."   Daniel

"If I had kids, at the moment they would not go to school. The structure of the system is unnatural and unjustifiable. It's forcing people to become clones of an idealised person. Even to rebel you have to do it in line with the stereotype. And they're bored at school. You've got to knock out of them the natural ability that they want to learn, because no teacher can look after 30 children all at different stages, all wanting to learn different things all at different times."   George

The one wholly home educated person who did not necessarily intend to home educate his own children was still determined to play a large part in their upbringing:

*"I'd love to say yes, but I don't think I've got the patience and dedication to home educate. I don't **think** I would. If my wife wanted to I'd support her fully. That's one of the reasons I'm trying to become successful early, so that when I'm thirty plus I can spend lots of time with the kids."*   Laurence

Thinking outside the box

Grand general conclusions have no place in a book of this kind, which has tried to show that the most effective, and most enjoyable, education is that which is unique to the needs and inclinations of the person who follows it.

It might be useful, though, to draw out some of the more interesting points by way of a summary:

Starting out

- more than half the parents educating at home were teachers who were disillusioned with school goals and methods
- offering children a choice was an important part of most parents' educational philosophy: this applied as much to going to school as to what activities they would undertake if educated at home
- relationships with the LEA were in most cases quite relaxed: many home educators found they could be helpful sources of ideas and materials

What they learnt and how they learnt it

- home educated children have much wider learning opportunities than are possible in school, and are able to get deeply involved in an activity because of the lack of artificial subject boundaries and time constraints
- this has particular benefits for creativity, which was an important part of most children's education
- the opportunity to come across new areas of interest, or links with existing ones, by chance, was widely valued
- there was an emphasis on talking as a learning tool as well as a way of developing articulacy and close family relationships

Resources, and how they were afforded

- parents were by no means the only teachers: many children taught themselves to a large extent; others found neighbours or friends who were practitioners in the skill they wanted to acquire

- finance was generally not a problem: families used their ingenuity to achieve their objectives, adapting resources or making use of college facilities for expensive exam subjects
- many parents had dropped out of conventional careers and were 'downshifters', leading a home-based working life into which the children's education naturally fitted

An old chestnut cracked

- all those interviewed were leading normal social lives as adults
- the vast majority had no problems making friends out of school or, if they went to it, at college
- those who had been entirely home educated had exceptional social skills and matured early, due to having mixed with people from a wide range of ages and backgrounds and having had the time and freedom to build a secure sense of identity
- many of the interviewees had taken on substantial voluntary work in the community
- the model of less authoritarian teacher/learner relationships could show the way to new developments in these roles in the next generation

Attitudes to work

- there was a huge variety in the forms of work interviewees had undertaken, with a slight bias towards the caring and creative areas
- many interviewees had found serious work in the adult world a useful part of their home education, from social, psychological and practical points of view
- most interviewees had tried their hand at lots of things - none had fixed ideas about a job for life, although most were committed to a particular field in which they wanted to work

Finally, some remarks on the interviewees' thoughts about their upbringing and the influence which these might have on society's attitude to the future of education. They were not dogmatic about home-based learning: none showed evidence of having been indoctrinated with anti-school propaganda. If they had arguments against conventional practice these were their own, the product of vigorous free thought, based, maybe, on later experience.

What they all have in common, whether planning home education or not, is that they take its existence as an option for granted. They know it is legal and viable and they understand some of the difficulties which can be involved. They talk about their own experiences to friends and colleagues, ensuring that others also know it is an option: education can be flexible, schooling can be dipped in and out of, or abandoned altogether. More families begin to think outside the box.

References and Recommended Reading

Adcock, J. (1994) *In Place of Schools*, London: New Education Press

Bendell, J. (1987) *School's Out - educating your child at home*, Bath: Ashgrove

Fogler, M. (1998) *Un-jobbing* Lexington, Kentucky: Free Choice Press

Goleman, D. (1995) *Emotional Intelligence*, London: Bloomsbury

Handy, C. (1994) *The Empty Raincoat*, London: Random House

Hemming, J. (1980) *The Betrayal of Youth*, London: Marion Boyars

Holt Associates (1997) 'Grown Homeschoolers Reflect on their School-free Lives', *Growing Without Schooling*, 118 Sept/Oct

Holt, J. (1974) *Escape from Childhood*, New York: Ballantine

Holt, J. (1982) *Teach Your Own*, Brightlingsea: Lighthouse Books

Holt, J. (1984 ed.) *How Children Fail*, Harmondsworth: Penguin

Holt, J. (1984 ed.) *How Children Learn*, Harmondsworth: Penguin

Holt, J. (1990) *A Life Worth Living - selected letters of John Holt*, ed. S. Sheffer, Ohio: State University Press

Holt, J. (1992) *Never Too Late*, Ticknall: Education Now and Lighthouse Books

Llewellyn, G. (1993) *Real Lives: eleven teenagers who don't go to school*, Eugene, Oregon: Lowry House

Meighan, R. (ed.) (1992) *Learning from Home-based Education*, Ticknall: Education Now

Meighan, R. (1993) *Theory and Practice of Regressive Education*, Nottingham: Educational Heretics Press

Meighan, R. (1997) *The Next Learning System: and why home-schoolers are trailblazers*, Nottingham: Educational Heretics Press

Shute, C. (1993) *Compulsory Schooling Disease: how children absorb fascist values*, Nottingham: Educational Heretics Press

Thomas, A. (1998) *Educating Children at Home*, London: Cassell

Webb, J. (1990) *Children Learning at Home*, Brighton: Falmer Press

Appendix

The Law

Parents' primary responsibility for their children's education is laid out in Section 7 of the 1996 Education Act (successor to the 1944 Act):

> *"The parent of every child of compulsory school age shall cause him to receive efficient full-time education suitable: (a) to his age, ability, and aptitude, and (b) to any special educational needs he may have, either by regular attendance at school or otherwise."*

A more detailed summary of the legal situation can be obtained from **Education Otherwise** (address below).

Useful organisations

(Enclose a C5 size SAE if you contact the British ones)

Education Now
113 Arundel Drive, Bramcote Hills, Nottingham. NG9 3FQ

Education Otherwise
P.O. Box 7420, London. N9 9SG (Helpline: 0900 151 8303)

Growing Without Schooling / Holt Associates
2380 Mass.Ave., Suite 104, Cambridge MA 02140. U.S.A.

Home Education Advisory Service
5 Elm Gardens, Welwyn Garden City, Herts. AL8 6RX

Human Scale Education
96 Carlingcott, Bath, Avon. BA2 8AW

Index